THE CAMPAIGN AGAINST
THE UNDERGROUND PRESS

THE CAMPAIGN AGAINST THE UNDERGROUND PRESS

Geoffrey Rips

Coordinator: Freedom to Write Committee

Foreword by Allen Ginsberg

•

**with reports by
Aryeh Neier
Todd Gitlin
Angus Mackenzie**

Edited by Anne Janowitz and Nancy J. Peters

CITY LIGHTS BOOKS
San Francisco

The Campaign Against the Underground Press
© 1981 by Geoffrey Rips

The Underground Press and Its Cave-In
© 1981 by Todd Gitlin

"Surveillance as Censorship" is reprinted
by permission of
Index on Censorship (London).
© 1981 by Aryeh Neier

"Sabotaging the Dissident Press" is reprinted
by permission of
the *Columbia Journalism Review.*
© 1981 by Angus Mackenzie

Library of Congress Cataloging in Publication Data

Unamerican Activities.
Includes bibliographical references.
1. Liberty of the press—United States.
2. Underground press—United States.
3. Government and the press—United States.
I. Rips, Geoffrey. II. Janowitz, Anne.
III. Peters, Nancy J.
PN4745.U5   323.44'5   81-6162
                               AACR 2
ISBN 0-87286-127-9

Designed by Nancy J. Peters

CITY LIGHTS BOOKS are edited by Lawrence Ferlinghetti
and Nancy J. Peters at the City Lights Bookstore,
Columbus at Broadway, San Francisco, California 94133.

CONTRIBUTORS

Geoffrey Rips is coordinator of the Freedom to Write Committee of PEN American Center. He is the winner of a 1979 CAPS grant for fiction. His fiction and poetry have appeared in New Directions 36 & *43; For Neruda, For Chile; Oxford Literary Review;* and *California Quarterly.* He has published articles in *Index on Censorship* and *The Nation.*

Todd Gitlin teaches sociology and mass communications at the University of California, Berkeley, and has written, among other books, *The Whole World is Watching: Mass Media in the Making and Unmaking of the New Left* (University of California Press, 1980).

Aryeh Neier has long been active in civil liberty campaigns. A Fellow of the New York Institute for Humanities, he has been the Executive Director of the New York A.C.L.U. and is on the editorial board of *The Nation.* His books include *Dossier* (1975), *Crime and Punishment: A Radical Solution* (1976), and a series of handbooks on rights of U.S. citizens.

Angus Mackenzie is a freelance writer in northern California. Editorial assistance was provided by Jay Peterzell of the Center for National Security Studies in Washington, which also provided research assistance. The article was financed in part by the Fund for Investigative Journalism.

Allen Ginsberg is an American poet, songster, pacifist, and teacher. Among his many books are *Howl, Kaddish, Mind Breaths*, and *The Fall of America*, which was given the National Book Award for Poetry. With Anne Waldman he co-founded the Jack Kerouac School of Disembodied Poetics at the Naropa Institute. He is a member of the National Institute of Arts and Letters.

PAGES FROM THE UNDERGROUND

CONTENTS

SURVEILLANCE AS CENSORSHIP
by Aryeh Neier

Censorship was a crucial issue to the framers of the United States Constitution and in 1791 they forbade it in the First Amendment. Political surveillance, on the other hand, as it is practiced in the twentieth century, was unknown until a decade or so after the First Amendment was incorporated in the American Constitution. The dubious distinction of inventing this essential tool of contemporary repression probably belongs to Napoleon's police master, Joseph Fouche. His spies (*mouchards*) kept the Consul, and then Emperor, informed of domestic unrest. Their techniques were remarkably similar to those used by police spies ever since, especially in their reliance on informers. Then as now, these informers included turncoats, infiltrators and, often, members of dissident groups blackmailed into informing.

To succeed at their task, informers are required to maintain their dissident status or to ingratiate themselves with those on whom they wish to inform by proving their radicalism. The police spy, therefore, often becomes an *agent provocateur*, entrapping the targets of surveillance into activities that provide a rationale for the state's punitive measures. Occasionally, the police spy becomes the organizer and perpetrator of the most serious conspiracies and crimes attributed to the dissidents—as happened with Mehée in Napoleonic France, with "Azev the spy" in Tsarist Russia and, most recently, in America, with Gary Thomas Rowe. An informer on the Ku Klux Klan for the Federal Bureau of Investigation (FBI), the story of Rowe's tangled career has not yet been fully unravelled, but it is now known that he committed some of the most serious crimes of violence against civil rights activists in the South in the 1960s, including murder.

Ironically, it was a descendant of Napoleon who first created the machinery for systematic political surveillance in the United States. On July 1, 1908, Attorney General Charles Joseph Bonaparte established within the United States Department of Justice a "Bureau of Investigation." It was not a popular move at the time and authorization for it probably could not then have been obtained from the United States Congress.

Investigation of crime was considered a matter for state and local police, and there were fears that a federal police agency would not confine itself to enforcement of the criminal law. A member of Congress from Iowa reflected the views of many of his colleagues when he said that, "No general system of spying upon and espionage of the people, such as has prevailed in Russia, in France under the Empire, and at one time in Ireland, should be allowed to grow up." (The reference to "France under the Empire" seems to have been a deliberate allusion to the Attorney General's ancestry.) But Bonaparte was able to establish the Bureau anyway because Congress had recessed for six months.

Until the United States entered World War I, Congressional opposition to political surveillance limited the Bureau to enforcement of federal laws regulating interstate crime, like auto theft and postal fraud. The war, which coincided with the Russian Revolution, inspired national hysteria over enemy spies and saboteurs (hardly any were ever caught), enemy aliens and, most of all, pacifist resistance at home to military conscription. The hysteria did not subside when the war ended; if anything it grew, fed by concern about the triumph of Bolshevism in Russia and by alarm over a series of anarchist bombings—some of them by letter bombs—in the United States. One victim of the bombings was a successor of Bonaparte as Attorney General, A. Mitchell Palmer, whose home was severely damaged, though no one was hurt.

In 1919, Attorney General Palmer established a General Intelligence Division (GID), or Radical Division as it was sometimes called, within the Bureau of Investigation. A 24 year old lawyer, J. Edgar Hoover, was placed in charge of the GID and quickly mounted a series of raids, known to history as "the Palmer Raids" of 1919 and 1920, in which between 5,000 and 10,000 suspected radicals were rounded up and jailed. Many were beaten and several hundred were deported, among them Emma Goldman, who was sent to the Soviet Union along with about 200 other deportees.

In 1924, Hoover was appointed to head the Bureau which subsequently acquired the name by which it is known today, the Federal Bureau of Investigation. By then, the post-World War paranoia about American Bolsheviks and anarchists had subsided a little and a new Attorney General, Harlan Fiske Stone, succeeded in directing Hoover to make the FBI concentrate its energies on law enforcement matters other than political surveillance. The slack was taken up, however, by local police departments, many of which had formed "red squads" during World War I.

The 1920s and 1930s were a period of political ferment and rapid social change in the United States. It was the era of the organization of industrial unions; of the Great Depression; of the migration of rural whites from the dust bowl states of the Midwest to the fertile valleys of the far West; of the migration of rural blacks from the agricultural South to the industrial North; and of the growth of movements that reflected and sometimes reproduced the ideological conflicts raging in Europe. The police red squads kept very busy monitoring all this activity, but with the FBI largely withdrawn from political surveillance, their activities were uncoordinated and there was no national repository of political intelligence data.

As tensions rose in Europe toward the end of the 1930s, Hoover's FBI began to get back into the political surveillance business. On September 6, 1939, a few days after Germany invaded Poland, President Franklin D. Roosevelt signed a directive on which Hoover continued to rely until his death in 1972 (at his death, he was still Director of the FBI, several successive Presidents having authorized him to stay beyond the normal retirement age) as the authority for the FBI to conduct political surveillance. In the directive, Roosevelt said that he was instructing "the Federal Bureau of Investigation to take charge of investigative work in matters relating to espionage, sabotage, and violations of the neutrality regulations" and it requested local police departments to turn over to the FBI any information they collected on these matters. The request to police departments also embraced "subversive activities."

While Roosevelt's directive was intended to deal with the wartime emergency, as far as Hoover was concerned the emergency never ended. World War II was followed by the Cold War and a new era of American hysteria about the threat of domestic subversion by reds. The FBI monitored the activities of the Communist Party, every group it suspected of being a front for the Party, and every group it suspected had been infiltrated by Communists. Anyone with even tangential contact with such a group became the subject of a dossier. Since the FBI files were augmented by reports from the red squads of police departments which continued to comply with Roosevelt's 1939 directive after the War ended, they grew voluminously. Millions of Americans became the subjects of FBI political dossiers during the post World War II era.

The late 1940s and the 1950s were also the era of government and industry sponsored "loyalty" programs in which tens of thousands of suspected subversives were denied jobs. A report in an FBI political dossier that an applicant for a government job (however remote from security matters) had attended a meeting of a group the FBI regarded as a Communist front was often sufficient to insure a rejection. It was the same in industries that held government contracts. In addition to getting information from the FBI, many industrial employers relied on dossiers by private loyalty investigation groups that did a thriving business selling such services.

Several other agencies of the federal government began collecting political dossiers during the Cold War era, among them the Central Intelligence Agency, the Internal Revenue Service, the Secret Service of the United States Treasury Department, the Immigration and Naturalization Service and the Passport Office of the State Department. Since this political surveillance was largely secret, it aroused little controversy. Public debate over surveillance centered on the entry into the field of several Congressional committees. Even today, when Americans think of political repression in the late 1940s and the 1950s, their thoughts focus on Senator Joseph McCarthy and on the House UnAmerican Activities Committee. McCarthy, in particular, gave his name to the era, "McCarthyism."

Congressional investigators like McCarthy relied heavily on FBI political dossiers in their exposés of Americans they accused of being Communists, "fellow travellers," "pinkos," "parlor pinks," "dupes" of Communists, members of Communist fronts, or participants in the activities of Communist fronts. Although millions of Americans were outraged by the likes of McCarthy, few worried as much about the FBI. The prevalent assumption among American political liberals in the 1950s was that the FBI must be far more professional than the clownish McCarthy. The FBI, so it was generally believed, could distinguish between genuine Communist spies and saboteurs, and the movie stars and college professors rightly or wrongly accused by the Congressional committees of such offenses as having taken part in a Communist front meeting twenty years earlier. Among liberals, it was popular in the 1950s to say that the Congressional investigations should be ended and the job of protecting the United States against subversion should be left to the FBI.

We know now that the FBI not only made it possible for the Congressional investigating committees to do their work but some of its own activities were worse than anything done by Senator McCarthy. In 1956, the FBI launched "COINTELPRO" (Counter Intelligence Program), a series of aggressive programs conducted for the next twenty years to disrupt the activities of certain organizations. In the 1950s the principal targets were left-wing groups such as the Communist Party and the Socialist Workers Party (a Trotskyist organization). In the 1960s, the FBI added as targets certain groups that it labeled as "White Hate Groups," "Black Nationalist Hate Groups" and the "New Left." The homes and offices of members of these groups were burglarized by the FBI. Informers for the FBI deliberately fomented feuds within these groups, sometimes by falsely portraying other members as informers, sometimes by arousing sexual jealousies, other times by false accusations of thefts of organization funds. And, the FBI entrapped members of some of these groups into committing crimes of violence. The feuds deliberately provoked by the FBI became serious enough to lead to some deaths — such as those resulting from the vendetta between the Eldridge Cleaver and Huey Newton branches of the Black Panther Party, a vendetta which FBI officials have boasted of creating.

During the 1960s, American preoccupation with the threat of subversion by domestic Communists diminished. Nevertheless, the FBI maintained its surveillance over them and other adherents of "Old Left" groups. To these it added surveillance of the "New Left" and of the millions of Americans who became active in protests against the war in Vietnam. When a rally against the war took place, the FBI tried to discover the identities of the participants by photographing them. It examined the bank accounts of antiwar groups to learn the names of contributors. It enlisted thousands of new informers — switchboard operators at colleges who listened in on the phone conversations of antiwar faculty members; postmen who noted the addresses on mailings from antiwar groups; even boy scouts, trained by the FBI to identify those suspected of harboring disloyal sentiments.

Authors of books and articles critical of the FBI and their publishers were special targets of Bureau surveillance and harassment. A prominent lawyer, Max Lowenthal, whose book *The Federal Bureau of Investigation* was published in 1950, was smeared as a subversive and FBI agents visited bookstores around the United States to get them not to stock the book. An informer's report (invented) that Lyle Stuart, publisher of a 1967 book critical of the FBI, was a "known homosexual who frequents midtown bars," was seized on gleefully by the Bureau's Director, J. Edgar Hoover. His handwritten note in the margin of the report instructing that the material should be disseminated, says "Good stuff!" When one of the best respected American journalists, Jack Nelson of the *Los Angeles Times* (now the newspaper's Washington bureau chief), wrote critical articles about the FBI, Hoover got in touch with his publisher Otis Chandler. In 1971, Chandler journeyed to Washington at Hoover's invitation to listen to the FBI Director read to him a series of reports purporting to describe Nelson's drinking habits. The episode did not persuade Chandler to abandon his support for Nelson. Other prominent journalists known to have been slandered for daring to criticize the Bureau include the late Alan Barth, editorial writer for *The Washington Post*; Fred Cook, a reporter who wrote frequently about the FBI for *The Nation*; James Wechsler, a columnist and former editor of the editorial page for *The New York Post*; and Harry Hoffman, editor of *The Charleston Gazette*.

Established journals survived the FBI's attack, though some muted their criticism of the Bureau. The effects on the lively "underground press" that flourished in the 1960s and the early 1970s were more serious. Harassed by local police departments as well as by the FBI, many closed down. A decade ago, virtually every sizeable American city in every state had at least one weekly newspaper that could be counted on to deal irreverently with public issues and cultural matters; today such newspapers survive in only a few of the largest cities on the East and West coasts.

It was a revelation in January, 1970, that the United States Army was compiling dossiers on the political beliefs and associations of Americans that finally made political surveillance a matter of great public controversy. The revelation came in a magazine article by Christopher Pyle, a lawyer and a former Captain in the United States Army. Pyle, who became an effective crusader against political surveillance, eventually persuaded more than a hundred former military intelligence agents to join him in revealing publicly that they had spied on the peaceful political activities of their fellow Americans. These revelations led to a new kind of Congressional investigation: instead of investigating Americans for harboring disloyal thoughts, a committee chaired by Senator Sam Ervin (who subsequently headed the Senate investigation of Watergate) investigated the agencies that conducted political surveillance. Pyle's revelations also led to an American Civil Liberties Union lawsuit against the United States Army charging that it had "chilled" the exercise of First Amendment rights of speech and association by the targets of its political surveillance.

Senator Ervin failed in his effort to get a law passed prohibiting domestic political surveillance by the military. And the ACLU lost 5-4 in the United States Supreme Court in 1972 in its effort to get the Court to declare that political surveillance violates the First Amendment. Even so, Pyle's revelations, Ervin's investigation and the ACLU lawsuit forced the military to end its political surveillance program. In the process, antagonists of surveillance learned something: like those who engaged in surveillance, they learned that the essential thing is to control information. If they could discover all that is done by those engaged in political surveillance and expose it to the light of day, the surveillance has to be discontinued. It can only operate effectively in secret.

In 1973, the Watergate scandal erupted and political surveillance was discredited by the revelations of Richard Nixon's ways of conducting it. Following Nixon's resignation in 1974, Congress adopted a Federal Privacy Act and amended the Freedom of Information Act. The effect of the two laws is to allow Americans to obtain copies of the political dossiers on them compiled by the FBI and other government agencies. In 1975, the CIA's political survellance programs were exposed publicly. Indeed, that year it seemed that hardly a day passed without some new revelation of government political surveillance. The practice was discredited as never before.

1975 to 1979 were thin years for political surveillance by American government agencies. That is not to say, however, that the practice is at an end. Private organizations took up some of the slack, just as local police departments took it up in the mid-1920s when the FBI temporarily withdrew under pressure from Attorney General Stone. In particular, private electric power companies that use nuclear energy have become heavily engaged in political surveillance. They justify the compilation of dossiers by the dangers to public safety if a terrorist organization was able to steal any of the plutonium that is used in a nuclear power plant or was able to blow up a plant. The large "anti-nuke" movement is the prime target of this political surveillance on the theory that such a terrorist group might emerge from within it. Other private companies also engage in political surveillance because of the fear that the terrorism prevalent in several European and Latin American countries might catch on in the United States. Groups antagonistic to big corporations, such as those concerned with consumer and environmental issues, are the leading targets of this surveillance.

An important factor in the shift of political surveillance to private corporations is that they are immune from disclosures under the Freedom of Information Act and to lawsuits alleging interference with constitutional rights. The United States Constitution only limits the government, not the activities of private corporations. And, several recent decisions by the United States Supreme Court have held that even private businesses that are actually quasi-public—like the electric power companies licensed and closely regulated by government—are nevertheless immune from constitutional restrictions.

In the past year, the possibility has arisen that government sponsored political surveillance will again achieve the proportions it reached before the exposés of the mid 1970s. A new mood prevails in the United States since the seizure of the American hostages in Iran and the Soviet Union's invasion of Afghanistan. One form it has taken is Congressional pressure on agencies like the FBI, which has been concentrating most of its energy lately on fighting organized crime and political corruption, to step up political surveillance. The greatest immediate danger is a powerful move to modify the Freedom of Information Act so that it could no longer be used to disclose information about the information gatherers. At this writing, it is not clear whether the Act will survive intact for another year.

The events of the past year make it plain that the struggle over political surveillance is far from at an end in the United States. Surveillance remains now what is has been for most of this century: the principal American way of political repression. While the absence of virtually all censorship keeps the United States free, it is through the practice of political surveillance that the United States most closely resembles the totalitarian nations of the world.

August 4, 1980

THE UNDERGROUND PRESS AND ITS CAVE-IN
by Todd Gitlin

Geoffrey Rips' report documents a myriad crimes of the State against free expression. The news is bad, important, and very much germane. The political consequences of these crimes persist. The criminals are at large, for the most part, and they are recovering their rationale for new adventures in mind policing. Yet in all the current outcry to get the government off the backs of the people, we do not hear official voices rising in righteous indignation against the crimes of official surveillance, harassment, and violence. That was the Sixties, wasn't it? Prevailing opinion would remind us again and again that the Sixties are long gone, and thank God for that. The Watergate burglary and its aftermath presumably purged the body politic of its foulest humors, its grossest wiretaps and crudest Plumbers. As a result of the civil libertarian purgation of the mid-Seventies, the Rockefeller Commission and Church Committee investigations and the safeguards that resulted—so says the New Right—the State now lies defenseless against its enemies, foreign and domestic, and is therefore entitled to recover its freedom of action against rambunctious journalists and other troublemakers. Rips' tales of a State run amok may therefore seem nothing more than what the Now culture derides as Ancient History.

We believe this at our peril. Like a deposed, cobwebbed statue of Stalin dragged out of storage, the old crimes and the old criminals are being resurrected. G. Gordon Liddy has become a folk hero of the lecture circuit, an object not only of curiosity but of admiration. Spy-chasers and would-be scourges of the Left are riding high in Washington again. A rejuvenated Senate Internal Security Subcommittee is mobilizing, and a best-selling novel (*The Spike*) is abroad in the land, adorned by Presidential recommendation, to justify insinuations that the legitimate research and publication offices of the Left are nests of espionage. In the early days of the Reagan administration, some officials were already floating trial balloons about restoring to the CIA some of its lost powers of domestic surveillance. Those particular balloons were quickly shot down, disowned by higher-ups in the Administration. The major newspapers were quick to take notice and offense: the Establishment press, though it has not been terribly interested in what the government was doing to the *underground* press, well remembers its own wars against the executive depredations of Nixon's time. But in the new Cold War mood, there will be other such balloons, and some of them will stay aloft. For the prolonged struggle against the Vietnam war has left this legacy at least: where there is a belligerent foreign policy, there will be popular resistance. And where there is popular resistance, there the apparatus of repression will recover from defeat and disuse, and swing back into motion, full of energies for hot and sloppy pursuit.

So this is a good time to learn some lessons from the stories Geoffrey Rips has compiled. It is a fine time to recall the dirty tricks, to feel indignant toward the violence done by the various goon squads of officialdom, and to renew our resolve that the State shall not be permitted to make the coming political opposition wither away. And it is also a good time to face, head on, the complexity of the Sixties. The underground press represented the best of the late-Sixties revolt, and its worst. I claim some experience, for in 1968 and 1969 I wrote regularly for the *San Francisco Express Times*, for many other underground papers via Liberation News Service, and for the *Guardian*. (Most of my examples will flow from the *Express Times*, where I worked eight or nine days a week.) The underground press was a political and cultural breakthrough; it was also replete with weaknesses and inanities. The underground press's own flaws in some ways allowed the State to make infiltration and repression work, to get away so easily with spiritual and sometimes corporeal murder. It is late in the game to rekindle a black-and-white romance about the underground press as an unsullied beacon of truth and innocence that got befouled by the State's under-handed agents of disinformation and suppression. Let's face it: the underground press bore the marks of the youth consciousness that nurtured it.

A romance it was, but no simple one. For writers, editors, photographers, artists, it was a marvelous adventure, full of infectious enthusiasm. With little money, less professional help or experience, we were improvising without blueprints, trying out unconventional forms of writing, learning design and layout and distribution as we went. On $40 a week—when it came—writers were staying up all night to do layout and set type. (Nobody did much bookkeeping.) Without a mainstream journalism to inspire us, we turned, cockily and half-consciously, to earlier generations of models, to the Orwell of *Homage to Catalonia*, the John Reed of *Ten Days that Shook the World*, to the pre-World War I *Masses* magazine of Max Eastman and Floyd Dell and Big Bill Heywood—if we turned to anyone. We were happy to be amateurs in the original sense, doing the work for love. Especially at first, the papers embodied the brave and winsome spirit of that moment, the audacity of breaking with old liberal and Marxist clichés alike, of setting out afresh to transvalue existing values and to clarify opposition to imperialism, racism, sexual hypocrisy, illegitimate authority of all kinds. We might have said what Sartre once wrote about his own generation: "We thought the world was new because we were new in the world." But our papers also embodied the desperado mood, the self-isolating truculence, the unexamined bravado, and, toward the end, the new wave of anti-liberal, right-on clichés of the movement that sustained it. Terrible beauties were born.

At their best, the papers were vibrantly alive, alert to the need to compose new syntheses between the New Left's political values—peace, national self-determination, equality, ecology—and some sort of cultural eruption. Just what kind was a problem to define well; whatever its confusion, this mass version of avant-garde culture was at least an attempt to get beyond the fatuity of commercial pap. But their major topics were directly political. They were publishing serious investigative work at a time when mainstream journalism was dead in the water. Along with the better-known *Village Voice* and the monthly *Ramparts*, they were steady outlets for news about Vietnam and Latin America, sympathetic to the Left but often sensitive to the Left's own controversies. (The *Express Times*, for example, printed three quite distinct reviews of *The Battle of Algiers* in a single issue, at a time when the film had become a cult totem on the Left.) The papers printed serious research—by movement networks like the North American Congress on Latin America and the Africa Research Group—into the institutions, byways and crannies of the imperium, exposing the doings of the Pentagon, the CIA, the police, the munitions-makers, and their corporate and academic allies: and this when the Establishment press was not yet inclined, even rhetorically, toward serious investigations into the scandals of the powerful. They regularly—if not analytically and not always reliably—reported on the black revolt, on GI movements and later, on the women's movement, on police strategies and attacks, most of it news which was not deemed fit to print in most respectable organs. They brought criticism of the war and sympathetic treatment of the antiwar movement to soldiers who had no other channels. They made public facts about the movement's growing net of community institutions, from co-ops to welfare organizations. They took the New Left seriously as something to write about, and, at their best, probed deeper than did the movement's own organizational sheets. They disdained hard-and-fast political or aesthetic lines.

And often they cared about good writing. Because their writers had not been schooled to death in any writing profession, they were free to seek—and sometimes to find—new angles. Although the papers were prone to self-justifying rhetoric and plain bad writing, they were often enough workmanlike in prose; and, more, hospitable to a range of styles and talents. The New Journalism really began in the underground, with first-person accounts of news events—demonstrations, press conferences, street scenes; writers began to treat their own notions and responses as part of the story, in revolt against the spurious objectivity of the mainstream. There was passion, flair, intelligence, fluidity, a chance for new writers to get out from under prevailing conventions of just-the-facts journalism (but *which* facts?) and stylized literary criticism (but of *which* texts?) There was even, miracle of miracles on the Left, a chance to escape the left-wing conventions of dullness, pontification, and capital-C Correctness. There was solid writing about rock music and film, about little theater and obscure books, about Italian markets (as Barbara Garson showed in the *Express Times*) or the anarchist theory of affinity groups (as Marvin Garson showed in the same place). Critics like Greil Marcus, fiction writers like Tom Farber, cartoonists like R. Cobb, photographers like Jeffrey Blankfort, essayists like Michael Rossman, investigative writers like Jeff Gerth, Lowell Bergman, and Danny Schechter—later at the *New York Times* and the network news organizations, respectively—these and other fine writers and artists first found publics through the best of the underground. And in layout and design, true, many papers belonged to the jumble school; in headlines, they lent themselves to sensation and scandal-mongering; but they were inventive in new tabloid formats, and there was much wit and much elegance too in the look. They were no strangers to wryness, were often funny and sometimes gorgeous. Not to mention how the papers enlivened the streets, made jobs for a host of street-sellers and, for a while, broke the lock of mainstream news distributors. Modernism in the streets, indeed.

But the whole story is always messy. The underground press was also puerile, devotedly adventurist, stupidly sexist, and childishly giddy about the revolutionary potential of drugs and the druggy potential of revolutions. But why? To comprehend the vulnerabilities of the underground press, we have to look to its crucible, the youth and student movements of the mid- and late Sixties. For the underground papers mirrored the confusions of the radical activists who edited and wrote for them; and those confusions were superimposed upon the muddle of the youth-culture city enclaves the papers served. From the early Sixties on, activists had tested their

rough ideas about radical change on a series of organizing ter-
rains—campuses, the rural South, black and white ghettoes.
In the process—and with the miserable war on—they were
evolving from disappointed radicals, hoping to redeem the
American dream, to would-be revolutionaries, caught up in
international solidarities, straining to improvise a radical
tradition and ideology. The campuses had been too confining,
organized liberals too retrograde, the ghettoes too hard to
organize; and then, in 1966, the blacks had thrown the whites
out of the civil rights movement, which had been one of the
New Left's major fields of action. What was to be done? As
activists came to feel more revolutionary—as if one could
simply declare oneself one by *feeling* that way!—we were running out of potential turfs. We lacked both strategy and a
sense of who could make this necessary and unprecedented
revolution; we were in a cul-de-sac disguised by passion. In
this mood, hundreds of organizers and activists discovered
the Protean, expanding youth enclaves that by 1966 and 1967
were settling into marginal neighborhoods in cities coast to
coast, harboring hippies, post-student dropouts, and a variety
of freaks and working-class and lumpen young. Could this be
the fabled new revolutionary constituency? At least this was
territory for political work. As Norm Fruchter later wrote, in
the most penetrating essay ever written about the underground press (and I've drawn heavily on it here: "Movement
Propaganda and the Culture of the Spectacle," *Liberation*,
May 1971), "Unsure about who to organize, how to organize,
on which constituencies to base oneself, unsure even about
the nature and legitimacy of one's own politics, thousands of
movement activists found they could participate only in the
writing, shaping, production and distribution of propaganda."

There was magic, as well as relief, when articulate young
radicals discovered the wonders—and the low costs—of weekly
offset printing. Thus the efflorescence of what came to be
called the underground papers, weekly or biweekly, hundreds
of them eventually, circulating from the low thousands to (in a
couple of cases) the hundreds of thousands, reaching what
must have been millions of readers regularly by 1970. But the
producers of these papers faced weekly decisions which were

not so different, in principle, from what the mass media confront: what to package to keep up not only circulation but their own interest. Driven to delusions about the revolutionary potential of the moment, the staffs resorted to sensationalism in order to hold the interest of a readership that was clearer about what it was not—straight, bourgeois, conservative—than about what it was, or wanted. They dispensed news of drugs, avant-garde versions of both genuine eroticism and collegiate smuttiness, and Left politics, piecing together a least common denominator.

By the late Sixties, desperation about the war and the police was fused with revolutionary fantasy. The cops were at the door but—or therefore—the revolution, whatever *that* was, was on the horizon. The nineteenth century's master metaphor of Progress alternated with the twentieth century's master metaphor of Doom: we were poised, in those years, between visions of World Revolution and Looming Fascism. "YEAR OF THE BARRICADES," the *Express Times* bannered, typically, one spring day in 1968, dreaming media-hyped dreams in the rosy afterglow of the revolt at Columbia University and the uprising in Paris. For the mass media were feeding the same mood, and giving starring roles to those in the movement who seemed Central Casting's gift to revolutionary imagery. The Bay Area's own street theatrics were readymade for two-color underground front pages depicting shadowy figures glimpsed through clouds of tear gas. In the spring of 1968, one exercise in seeming insurrection succeeded another. One week it was Berkeley students and street people protesting the City's refusal to close the streets for a demonstration in solidarity with the French students and workers; the next it was a teeny-bopper riot in suburban Pacifica, with the *Express Times* headlining, "PACIFICA: REVOLUTIONARY SURPRISE!"

Well, none of these exercises in insurrection was made up; *this all happened*. But beneath the surface of uprisings of the week, the movement, and the underground papers with it, were lurching into a manic-depressive cycle. As lost in political smoke as the rest of the Left—and liberals too, for that matter—most underground papers overrode their own deep perplexity by devoting themselves, progressively, to street-wise machismo, to pronunciamentos from Eldridge Cleaver and other Black Panther leaders, and from Jerry Rubin, Abbie Hoffman, Timothy Leary, and many local versions. Indiscriminately, each of these foreshadowed one or another apocalypse which, God knows, there seemed good reason to credit. It was a heady mixture. Editors more than half-believed their own headlines. The papers were becoming drugs for rising giddiness, balms for the widely felt but intractible despair and sense of irrelevance. Consider for a moment the fact that in November of 1968, for example, just as the nation in its unwisdom prepared to elect Richard Nixon president of the United States, SDS, the major student organization of the New Left, was deluding itself that mass demonstrations were a popular alternative to mere voting. The *Express Times*, to name only one paper—and one of the most sophisticated—was cracking bad phallic jokes about Erection Day. Meanwhile, the enemy was too easy to recognize: Them, the Combine, the Straights, the Imperialists, . . . and, increasingly, the Pigs.

Faced with a monstrous and seemingly unstoppable war, and lacking much clear political identity or self-understanding, the papers, with noble exceptions, slipped into traps. Learning politics fast, and without much tutelage, they slid toward *postures* more than developed *politics*, toward a kind of instant anti-imperialism. If you couldn't tell the players without a scorecard, the papers would give their readers a scorecard: good guys with their youth and organics, bad guys with their napalm and conspiracies. The papers became cheerleaders for the approved revolutionary nations—Cuba, North Vietnam, China, sometimes North Korea. (But not, crucially, the later murderous and totalitarian Khmer Rouge of Cambodia, who were manufactured, for the most part, by the American bombing of that miserable land, and never romanticized by the Left.) Bending over backwards to avoid any taint of racism, these white-controlled papers contorted themselves into uncritical embrace of Third World heroes. It was almost impossible to resist. When the police were gunning down a string of Black Panthers, culminating in the Chicago police murder of the extraordinary leader Fred Hampton, few writers on the

Left wished to devote their investigative energies to uncovering skeletons in the closets of the righteous. The trap was to succumb to thought-loops, self-censorship, believing too much of your own cant. In a society saturated by media images, what was real anyway? Why not revolution? Never mind that there was no constituency for it, no strategy for it, and not much its partisans could say to recommend it to the unconvinced.

And if heroes could legitimately be found among the Vietnamese—a small nation taking the heaviest bombardment of all time, and successfully fighting back!—they could also be found among our own. In a society which, for the first time in the history of the world, numbered more college students than farmers, a society which worshiped youth and its commodities, it was easy, under pressure, for the youth culture to get carried away with a sense of political possibilities unlimited. If the media, the police, and the prosecutors treated you as dangerous revolutionaries, maybe, by God, you really were. In 1969, for example, the *Berkeley Tribe*—a staff-run split-off from the famous *Barb*—featured on its cover a photo of a hip couple, one with rifle in hand, the other with baby on back, striding purposefully toward the sheltering woods. There were so many freaky-looking people styling themselves outlaws— and often enough being treated as such by straight society— it was possible to think of this movement *itself* as the revolution in embryo: or more fancifully, as the late Marshall Bloom, co-founder of Liberation News Service, put it to me in all seriousness once, as an artificial peasantry which would populate the wide-open American countryside and serve as a social base for the nonviolent guerrillas of the future. This was a time when serious activists organized gun clubs and studied the Chairman's Little Red Book for pearls of metaphysics as well as political wisdom. Karate was a more popular pursuit than the study of political economy. It sounds funny now, but this was very much the mood that radiated through the underground press and the larger movement in the late days of the decade. The more frenetic, the more isolated.

And at the same time, the papers were also soaked in unexamined sexism, and sexism played no small part in undermining their precarious balance. Locker-room stuff that might have passed in 1965 would not pass in 1968 or 1969. In 1968, for example, an *Express Times* writer interviewed a female antiwar activist who had just come back from Hanoi accompanying released American POWs. The writer was a hip guy who wrote a brilliant personal prose; he was in the habit of writing brash and writing confessional, and sometimes without being sure which was which. And so he featured in his piece, complete with graphic metaphors, the fact that he was lusting for the subject of his interview. Bay Area women activists were, of course, enraged. So, it has to be said, were many men; several *Express Times* writers published their own protests. But I mention this incident simply to suggest how unthinking, at times, was the sexism of the underground press. It is also true, as Angus Mackenzie reports in a valuable article ("Sabotaging the Dissident Press," *Columbia Journalism Review*, March/April 1981), that when the FBI successfully leaned on Columbia Records to stop advertising in underground papers, they left the papers little choice but to become economically dependent on smarmy sex ads. As in the mainstream media, editors everywhere were almost entirely male, and they were slow to comprehend the rising tide of women's anger against male supremacy. By the early Seventies, on some staffs, women were organizing, denouncing the men, even booting out male editors entirely. As in the movement at large, their rage at the men erupted so profoundly because these were *their* men, the men who talked a good game about equality, the men from whom better was expected.

So, to sum up: by 1969, revolutionism and internal contradiction had stretched the underground press to a breaking point. As circulation and political hopes swelled, so did internal fragility. The point of my notes is not that anyone then knew how to conduct mass insurgent politics with greater finesse or intelligence; in my view, no one did. But the fact remains that the kicky, pungent underground press was altogether too cavalier about offending liberal and possible working-class allies. As things developed, "freaks" and "politicos" grew polarized; and divided houses were especially vulnerable to FBI provocations and dirty tricks. All these tensions were there to be exploited by government meddling.

I don't think we yet know the full dimensions of the damage the State did. Take, for example, its role in the factionalism that tore apart Liberation News Service. In 1967 and 1968, LNS was a lively and diverse feature service, shipping weekly packets of news reports, reviews, interviews and commentary to scores and, eventually, hundreds of subscribing papers and radio stations (not to mention, it turns out, a few FBI informants). Geoffrey Rips points out that the FBI meddled in LNS's split in 1968, when the "freaks" took off to the Massachusetts countryside and the "politicos" stayed in New York. For a while there were two different LNS mailings going out, LNS-Mass. and LNS-NY. Perhaps the Feds were involved in the hardening of both positions; it would not have been the first time the government had a hand in the excesses, even the crimes, of ultras. In any case, the split worked to the detriment of both sides. Dissension of this sort damaged political morale, even good judgment, throughout the world of the underground press. Nerves frayed; trust melted. It is hard to say what specific effect the FBI and other State agencies had on all this—what part they played in provoking some of the papers' standardized Third Worldism, street-tough flamboyance, drug-dependence. But certainly the government goon squads polluted the political atmosphere.

And certainly they did other direct injuries. As Rips makes abundantly clear, official violence and intimidation took their toll in several cities. Set-up drug busts, even physical assaults against reporters (as in San Diego, Dallas, and Houston), helped drive some papers out of business, and made it hard to recruit new talent. The FBI helped drive nervous advertisers away, and intimidated printers and street sellers.

The worst of it is that we don't know what the underground press might have become. For all their immaturity, the papers did yeoman service in opening up the country's politics and culture. Had they been given a chance to develop along their own course, they might have outgrown their infancy. Stupid factionalism might have been overcome. Where fissures had formed, bridges might have been built.

But intimidation and harassment work by choking off

open futures. When the State comes off its leash, it does not care about fine distinctions. It aims to oversimplify, to deform and destroy. We delude ourselves if we think that the heavy-handed de facto censors of the repressive State would behave more delicately toward a more discreet opposition, or one with clearer politics. Their interest is not in encouraging coherent political thinking, but in smothering any real challenge to the established order. That is why civil libertarians must stay vigilant against the chill. Toward that end, Geoffrey Rips' report is a valuable unearthing, and an apt warning.

April 1981

SMOKING TYPEWRITERS
by Allen Ginsberg

"What is now proved was once only imagined."
— *William Blake*

The reader of this PEN Freedom to Write Committee document on government harassment and attempted destruction of the underground press will glimpse only the top of the pile of press clippings, court records, word-of-mouth testimony & anecdote, vast rooms full of FBI files & Congressional hearings, whole libraries that substantiate the cases cited, and document them hundred-fold in detail & gruesome effect.

Tho the account compiles reliable data on harassment, arrests, beatings & jailings of journalist-citizens, trials & much waste of money on unconstitutional prosecution of workers in dissenting media, it should be clearly stated that not one agent of the government engaged in these nationwide criminal (legally illegal) activities has ever been punished by jail, and very few by prosecution. Two heads of the FBI involved with these nefarious terrorisms who were tried and convicted for only one obvious case of illegal surveillance among the many crimes committed (in this instance, harassment of ill-mannered Weatherman groups) were immediately pardoned in 1981 by the very President whose conservative campaign philosophy promised to "get the government off our backs."

If the secret police bureaucracies of the government, illegally operating to torment and terrorize legal dissenters, are not precisely those bureaucrats who should be kept off our backs, then what is meant by this pious slogan? Our Bill of Rights was adopted to limit the pushiness of such police spies, government gossips, agents-provocateurs, kinky bureaucrats, and double agents who smoke pot & lush, scream "pig," & then try to frame idealistic citizens for the same crimes they are hired to commit. Such "COINTELPRO" Terrorism is, after all, an invention of the police in all countries, including U.S.A.

What ignorant hypocrisy has so reversed conventional usage that now citizenly Thoreauvian pacifism (i.e. nonviolent antinuclear action) has been called "terrorism" and actual government-inspired bombings, beatings, thievings & lies have been excused by the President of the U.S. as patriotic action "on high principle" in pursuit of government interest?

What hypocrisy this presidential actor dares display to a large minority of affronted citizens. How many see thru this Orwellian twist of language that says "War is Peace"? Government terrorism is "Internal Security," and "Get the government off our backs" are buzzwords for increasing the Military Bureaucracy and for turning the government treasury into a pig's trough of military expenditures.

How dare the aboveground press of America allow this continuous hoax to maintain itself, like a public hallucination, a doublebind extreme enough to freak the entire nation into schizophrenic crime in the streets—one half of the brain screaming No More Government Interference in the Private Sector! & the other half yammering for More Military! More Electric Police! More Funds for the Pentagon's Brass Bands! The chutzpah of those scholars of war who chatter endlessly their priggish syntax in praise of a "free market" of goods & ideas! Half the national budget enslaves us for life behind the bureaucratic iron of a Military Industrial Reformatory equipped with radioactive showers.

Who had the guts & courage to see this Imperial Roman fraud for what it was and protest out loud? The Underground Press among others. Who served it up in the language of the people, private news of civilization's waste, terrible news for youth, not "fit to print" in middleclass media that for generations had averted eyes from domestic race bloodshed, sex persecution, political persecution, eyes glazed over with American Imperial Murder in Latin America, yet hypnotized by Red Imperial Murder in Siberia? The Underground Press saw that much.

While J. Edgar Hoover denied for decades the existence of organized crime, he devoted the energies of his intelligence agency to eavesdropping on Martin Luther King, Jr.'s bedrooms and to myriad-paged surveillance of white negro Abbie Hoffman's psycho-political gaga. This sex blackmailer and dryhanded public virgin was lunching secretly each week with the East Coast spokesman for organized crime, Frank Costello, in N.Y. Central Park's Tavern on the Green (according to the *Time* magazine obituary).

Take a look at the documents reproduced in this PEN report—a plan to cut down the charismatic influence of black leaders and organizations including the Student Non-Violent Coordinating Committee & Nobel Peace Prizewinner Martin Luther King, Jr., A 12 point plan to ridicule, misinform, blackmail, dissolve, destroy, discredit, infiltrate, jail and make ugly images of the bewildered New Left and its shoestring press. A plan to set black man against white man. After you have read these FBI documents you realize that all through the Sixties the notion of Race Separation and Race Nationalism— "Tough bad Blacks can't work with punk Liberal Whites"— was escalated by FBI double agents & poison-pen letter-writers and orchestrated to produce national paranoia. What are we to say of these criminals paid by FBI, state and local Red Squads? What are we to say to their bewildered victims? How can we console a stunned generation of scared 80's kids, Punk New Wave Conservative alike, stereotyped as incapable of political action because they saw in the "friendly mass media" "obnoxious" photos of peace protestors? ("Naturally, the most obnoxious pictures should be used.")

What to say to the millions of blacks who've known all along—moaned and wept under the August 25, 1967 "COINTELPRO" plan to deprive them of their political consciousness, their constitutional rights of assembly, their press, and some of their leadership?

Why did the FBI lay off the Mafia and instead bust the alternative media, scapegoating Poet Leroi Jones, ganging up on Jane Fonda, Tom Hayden, M. L. King, Jr., anti-war hero Dave Dellinger, even putting me on a Dangerous Subversive Internal Security list in 1965—the same year I was kicked out of Havana & Prague for talking and chanting back to the "Communist" police?

"The fox condemns the trap, not himself," Blake wrote in *Proverbs of Hell*. Remember that Mr. Gallup, our national pollster, reported back in 1968 that the majority (52%) of the nation did feel that the Vietnam War "all along had been a mistake." This tipping of the national mind balance occurred just at the time U.S. police networks were teletyping out their August 5, 1968 grand master plan for counterintelligence to disrupt the New Left Coalition and press opposed to an undeclared war—a war which ended exploding more bombweight than all previous modern wars and crippled Indochina for the rest of the XX century. Then America had its nervous breakdown, the 1970s.

If America goes more Totalitarian (and we've got a good beginning, for a bunch of jerks who advertise ourselves as the "Free World"), won't it be because the media allowed sadistic police hypocrites to stink-bomb & beat up spokesmen for a majority of the U.S. populace?

Poet Robert Duncan observed that under the mask of American violence lies all the grief we feel for our "unacknowledged, unrepented crimes."

"Slowly the poison the whole bloodstream fills;
The waste remains, the waste remains and kills."
— William Empson

This document can enlighten the Establishment in America as to a cause of its own grief. The Federal, State, and local Police Bureaucracy censored the youthful frankness of the Alternative Press. W. S. Burroughs (an American novelist widely published and interviewed for decades in the underground media) remarks: "What the American alternative press did in the 1960's under considerable pressure is of inestimable value. Many of the gains in freedom that we take for granted in the 1980's were won due, in great part, to the efforts of the alternative press—among others: 1. Ending of Vietnam War. 2. Decriminalization of marijuana. 3. Abolition of Censorship. 4. Recognition (if not complete realization) of minority rights. Poets, Writers, journalists, editors, and publishers—all did their work in a concerted effort." There was an international breakthru of cultural insight in the'60s that amounted to a World Revelation. The "Youth Movement" came out on the streets not only in New York, Chicago, and San Francisco but also in Singapore, Budapest, Belgrade, Paris, London, in cities on both sides of the Iron Curtain.

A 1984 American generation may glimpse here the trauma and jail-helplessness, the unconscious blood-fear they've inherited, that's hexed many a mouth to imitate the same bland singing-in-the-dark doubletalk they hear on commercial television in the course of being sold more gasoline war.

June 17, 1981, Boulder, Colorado

Special thanks to Attorney Ira M. Lowe, Esq., for his prophetic accuracy in legal pursuit of literarily related Freedom of Information Act files thru all secret branches of the government.

THE CAMPAIGN AGAINST
THE UNDERGROUND PRESS

by
Geoffrey Rips

NOTE
by Geoffrey Rips

In the mid-1970s, Allen Ginsberg, a member of PEN American Center's Freedom to Write Committee, suggested that it look into rampant government sabotage of the underground press movement. Most of PEN's 1500 members were aware of intelligence agency abuses but not of their extent. Because the Freedom to Write Committee works on behalf of imprisoned writers and censored writing around the world, it agreed to investigate if Ginsberg would provide the evidence he had amassed. Between 1968 and 1972, he had been collecting newspaper clippings, letters, and sworn affidavits from those who had been harassed, as well as files obtained through the Freedom of Information Act. People sent him reports of incidents, which they sometimes regarded as curious, sometimes as sinister; however, when assembled, they formed a pattern of systematic abuse. Ginsberg put this information at the disposal of the Freedom to Write Committee, which asked me, in 1979, to gather more information and write this report.

I would like to thank many people for their assistance: Allen Ginsberg; Dore Ashton and the Freedom to Write Committee; Karen Kennerly, PEN Executive Director; Bob Rosenthal; Ira Lowe; Jerry Simon Chasen; Marty Lee of the Assassination Information Bureau; Craig Silver of the Alternative Media Syndicate; the Fund for Open Information and Accountability, Inc.; Michael Ratner of the Center for Constitutional Rights; the Center for National Security Studies; the Campaign for Political Rights; Chip Berlet; Ms. magazine; Lucien Carr; Ellen Binder; Nancy Maniscalco; and Nancy J. Peters and Anne Janowitz of City Lights.

This book is dedicated to writing judged unfit to print in The New York Times. *It is dedicated to the anarchic, rawboned prose of investigative reporters not content with the information in press releases, to those journals so economically vulnerable that they were supported by their workers. It is dedicated to the writers, editors, artists, designers, distributors, and sellers, who worked day and night on antiquated, broken-down equipment, who wondered if the phones were tapped and why the mail never arrived, whose cameras were smashed, who went to jail.*

This book is dedicated to the memory of William B. Schanen, courageous printer and publisher, to the memory of D. A. Levy, poet and editor of The Buddhist Junkmail Oracle, *to the memory of George Jackson, to the memory of Tom Forcade, to the memory of Daniel DesRoches.*

This book is written for the sounding of the "barbaric yawp over the roofs of the world."

DISSIDENT VOICES

Washington Free Press, "early October," 1969.
U.S. imperialism depicted as a national addiction.

DISSIDENT VOICES

In the 1960s, investigative journalists, poets, novelists, political activists, community organizers, and artists formed an unprecedented alliance for change in the vigorous underground press movement that flourished in the United States. This network of counterculture, campus, and other alternative media brought larger political issues into communities, awakening citizens to their own power to influence national policy.

Surprisingly, the rapid growth in the number of underground newspapers and readership was mirrored by a sudden, equally rapid, decline in the early 1970s. The fate of the underground press followed that of the Movement, in general. The end of that great incubator of dissent, the Vietnam War, and the dismantling of the draft reduced the sense of immediacy felt by many people. Disagreements over strategy and goals fragmented the nascent New Left. While alternative journals belonging to the older traditions of muckraking, Left political commentary and party papers survived into the 1980s, the self-supporting, community-based underground press began to lose the vast number of readers it had once attracted. Many papers simply couldn't make it financially in the increasingly apathetic 1970s. Others were gradually taken over by commercial interests, which, having discovered a new market for records, drug paraphernalia, and fashions, thrived on advertising revenues and diluted political content.

The dramatic decline of the underground press has been attributed to many things. The end of the war and a changing

kaleidoscope

VOL. 1 NO. 13   APRIL 26 – MAY 9, 1968   25¢

V. D. REPORT P. 2   BLUE MOVIES   P. 16
CARMICHAEL   PRESS CONFERENCE   P. 15

member: underground press syndicate (u.p.s.)   milwaukee,
liberation   news   service   (l.n.s.)   wisconsin

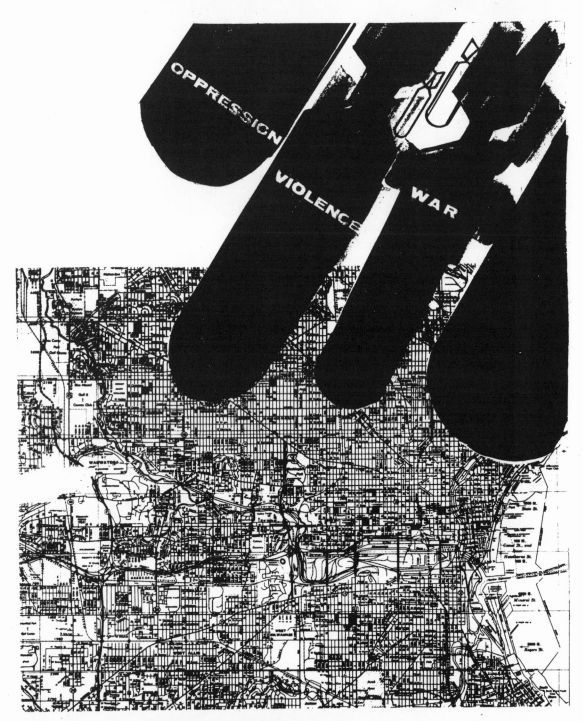

NATIONAL STRIKE; APRIL 26 See Story on P. 3

economy were critical factors; and the inexperience, bad management, self-indulgence, and political naiveté that plagued many alternative journals cannot be overlooked. But most of these analyses omit one ominous fact: the withering of the underground press was not entirely a natural decline. Alternative presses, whether serious journals of adversary politics or counterculture avant-garde papers, were targets of surveillance, harassment, and unlawful search and seizure by U.S. government agencies. Operating with pragmatic immorality, these agencies were mobilized to crush the constitutional rights of a large sector of the American populace which had found it necessary to dissent.

The freedom of expression and the freedom of the press have always been relative freedoms. A government intent on controlling the economic and social realities of a country must understandably become involved in the manipulation of the written perception of those realities, even at the expense of legal and moral principles held to be the cornerstone of that government. Dissenters from the British Crown founded this country and wrote into its Constitution provisions to ensure free discussion of the public good. The First Amendment is explicit: "Congress shall make no law . . . abridging the freedom of speech or of the press." This is a liberty heralded as a model for the rest of the world. Although it is not customary to associate the American experience with police and military action against writers, our press liberties have always been in jeopardy. Government surveillance of political and cultural expression has existed here not only for decades but for centuries. The re-affirmation of these freedoms by one generation seems to be either taken for granted or forgotten by the next. The suppression of press freedom during the McCarthy era was not an aberration of the 1950s as some recent films and articles suggest.

Now, once again, revelations about government interference are awakening a new awareness of a need for vigilance. During the 1960s and 1970s, the U.S. Government, through its police and surveillance agencies, made a full-scale effort to silence dissident writing and publishing. Under at least three administrations, it developed highly sophisticated techniques

Students for a Democratic Society   1608 West Madison   Chicago, Illinois

SDS NEW LEFT NOTES

Vol. 4, Number 6   LET THE PEOPLE DECIDE   February 1969

NIC notes

(See Page 9)

Huey rallies to stress self-defense

SDS and the Black Panther Party will celebrate Huey P. Newton's birthday (Feb. 17) at rallies across the country. The theme will be the Panther concept of self-defense based on the active participation of the community in its own protection. The rallies can also be used as part of a program to attack institutional racism, and can serve as an occasion to help build a working relationship with the Panthers on local levels. The NIC last weekend voted to encourage SDS chapters to participate in rallies, or sponsor them alone if there is no local active black group. (For related stories, see pages 6 and 7.)

People's Republic of China/LNS

NEW LEFT NOTES
Room 206
1608 West Madison Street
Chicago, Illinois 60612

RETURN REQUESTED
Second-class postage
rate paid in Chicago,
Illinois

Chicago Grand Jury

(The grand jury looking into Chicago's Democratic Convention demonstrations has leaked its plans to indict at least six movement people, probably under the federal interstate riot act. It's important that we know how to meet this latest attack on us. See story on page 3.)

1. IF YOU ARE SUBPOENAED TO APPEAR BEFORE THE GRAND JURY, NOTIFY US AT ONCE. YOU NEED LEGAL COUNSEL.

2. IF YOU KNOW OF OTHER PEOPLE WHO HAVE BEEN SUBPOENAED ALSO CONTACT US AT ONCE.

to intimidate the press that spoke for the popular liberative movements of recent decades.

In the past twenty years, the consolidation of domestic and international intelligence networks, the increasing feudal power of the multinational corporations, and the predominance of recording tape, the computer, and the silicon chip have brought a new sophistication to the control of the written word. Because the silicon chip can store vast quantities of information, printed matter can be scanned and analyzed for "sedition" with great speed and little labor. A more subtle kind of control takes place too. With the sheer mass of information available to media, censorship has come to operate by simply excluding what is aberrant. The marginal economic nature of underground newspapers and the "marginal news" they carried—often considered not "fit to print" by established dailies—rendered them particularly vulnerable to government persecution because they were considered outside the limits of polite society and, therefore, not worthy of the constitutional guarantees afforded established writers and publications.

Whether or not they were affiliated with specific political formations, people drawn to underground papers were activists against the war in Southeast Asia, and many also worked with programs for social reforms, or on behalf of oppressed groups such as women, blacks, or gays. The government was first alerted to the political implications of the underground press movement through its surveillance of maverick cultural and political movements. Its interest in underground writing intensified when a nation-wide network of alternative media began speaking to and for a largely youthful counterculture that troubled those in power by raising urgent issues untouched by the commercial media.

Small journals began springing up all over the country. They had much in common: they opposed the Vietnam war, advocated sexual and artistic freedoms, and urged critical consciousness towards conventional authority and power relations. Some called for communal or cooperative living; and many warned of the dangers of uncontrolled technology, especially nuclear power. Poetry, prose, graphic arts, and coverage

The Now Yerk Times

"All the News That's Fit to Print" VOL. CXVII By Dick Preston

PRESIDENT URGES MARINES KILL 162 STARTING MONDAY

Toll in '68 Rises to 2,242—Saigon Toll Not Disclosed—Other Allies Lose 18

TAX BENEFITS PROPOSED

Says Ambassador Met King on Day of Coup Attempt

PAPERWORK LAG IS CITED

By ROY DANZIG
Special to The New York Times

AUSTIN, Tex., Feb. 22—President Johnson, reflecting the national concern with decaying cities, outlined today a broad public-private plan for rebuilding the residential hearts of the nation's urban centers.

"You send the best of this country off to be shot and maimed," she said. "They rebel in the street. They will take pot and they will get high. They don't want to go to school because they're going to be snatched off from their mothers to be shot in Vietnam."

No Casualty Figures Released

Official casualty figures have not been released, but the battallion is known to have suffered about 50 dead and at least 200 seriously wounded. A marine battalion normally has 1,200 men, but the number can vary according to the unit's mission.

Emergency contracts are actually work orders that do not require competitive bidding. They can be issued by most of the city's commissioners. The necessity for quick repairs of things like broken water mains—demand their.

One company was withdrawn from the line today with only 61 men left. A Marine company at full strength comprises 205 men.

Another company in combat until the end was down to 71 men. One fresh Marine company was brought in last night.

Tall, urbane, impeccably dressed, with the kind of firm-jawed good looks popularized in old Arrow collar ads, he mined New York from its upper social stratum—where sabled matrons and their bewattled

Professor Giving Lesson With Simple Mortar

Only 15% Friends and Enemies Expect Answers to Religious Questions to Call In the Common Core by Midsummer

According to a poll of 1,010 persons conducted for The New York Times, 59 per cent of the state's citizens sided with the population. And there are plainly fears and prejudices in areas with a heavy colored population, notably in the sort of Midlands industrial area caused "by Kenya Government pressure against non-African holding jobs and by political speeches in Britain pressing for a barrier."

"A ragged old peasant will walk up to an installation to ask for a handout," one United States source said, "but under his breath, he's counting—171

His voice is often tinny and high-pitched, as if it were being projected by a cheap tape recorder. In fact, he makes sure there is always a tape recorder running whenever he speaks—"to preserve the wisdom," an aide explained.

Further signs of uneasiness were provided yesterday when Prof. Ota Sik, the nation's chief economic reformer, contended in a radio interview that workers had been told not to accept the reforms because they would lose their "privileges."

"If the race goes too slowly, then Eddie, he'll be in bad shape," said Grignola, a small, 33-year-old former driver, who wears a peaked cap and a worried expression. "The horse has the big heart—he only wants to go fast!"

The United States Embassy reported that 27 American civilians had been killed since the offensive began and that 17 were listed as missing. Three of these civilians are believed to be prisoners.

Although the Mayor took the harder line against the sanitationmen's union, he nevertheless

Continued on Page 26, Column 1

U.S.-SOVIET DRAFT TO SHUT AT 2 P.M. BUT FOE FIGHTS ON

Right to Strike Except for Health and Safety Units

Gift From New Canaan

A $50 check arrived anonymously from a New Canaan, Conn. donor, in memory of his mother "who never missed a year" as a contribution to your good work.

While he was in the room, however, Miss Kitt stood up and asked him, "What do you think about delinquent parents, parents who can't spend time with their children?"

President Replies

The President, taken aback by the unexpected question, said that day care centers had been established under Social Security legislation and added, "I think it would be a good idea if you would ask the women and then tell me what you think."

He left soon afterward.

"I was shaken and confused," he said "by militant Buddhist leaders who said that they oppose the South Vietnamese Government, but yet do not think that the United States

NARCOTICS RAID AT BUFFER ZONE

Education Board, 'Shocked' Says Johnson's Address, Shows Aim Isn't Peace

Indefinite LSD Sentences

WASHINGTON, Jan. 18 (UPI)—President Johnson will ask Congress to permit judges to sentence LSD pushers to indefinite prison terms, an Administration official said today.

Four college girls said yesterday they knew of students, who pooled their money to help pay for abortions for co-eds in need.

Side by side, the two shows present a surprising sociological paradox in which expected roles are being reversed. Some are digging around the roots while others are more anxious to cultivate the branches.

The findings may also help to establish guidelines for anti-smoking efforts directed toward youngsters.

Police and military personnel are believed to be participating in these clandestine operations, either directly or in the ranks of the right-wing groups, notably one known as La Mano

Mrs. Lyndon B. Johnson and Eartha Kitt at the White House luncheon yesterday before Miss Kitt's tirade. The singer denounced the Administration's Vietnam vehicle after the soldier was struck by fragments from an enemy rocket recent action took place about 70 miles north of Saigon, less than a mile from Cambodian Chief of State, in a review of an honor guard after his arrival at bookcases are nearly empty and an American flag stands forlornly in the Freighters unloading into lighters in Saigon Harbor. Some of thousands of tons of supplies winds up on the black market. Some even falls into enemy hands.

Screen: The Death of a Draft Dod

An Underground Elegy, Special Alert to 130,000—

By RENATA WILLIAM

"WINDFLOWERS," which opened yesterday at the underground New Cinema Playhouse, is a movie by Adolfas Mekas (who directed "Hallelujah the Hills") and declined to name the communities that had ordered the equipment.

"It's ticklish business," said William Moore, general manager of the company, "and everyone who has ordered cars has asked us not to disclose their names."

About 100 marines have been killed since Jan. 2. The airstrip in the mountain valley, the garrison's lifeline, is under such constant shellfire that planes do not dare to come to a full stop while unloading men and supplies. Whether they use them as sedatives, for weight control or to get high is irrelevant."

U.S. MARINES GAIN STOCK EXCHANGES

Its Meat Law Here

"The Now Yerk Times" collages the news "fit to print."
By Dirk Preston. *East Village Other.*

of folk and rock music thrived in the underground. And these popular arts swelled the rising tides of dissent.

Political information supplied by independent news services, such as the Liberation News Service and the Underground Press Syndicate, usually differed greatly from that offered by establishment media, which often relied heavily on government and Pentagon sources. Just as alarming to Washington may have been the close connections between alternative media and independent community action. Many of the underground papers worked closely with daycare centers, free medical clinics and food cooperatives. Others were connected with movements to extend social democracy and with insurgent political parties. The Black Panther Party, for example, initiated school breakfast and neighborhood defense programs. These and other issues vital to blacks were discussed in its *Black Panther Party Paper*. Members of the White Panther Party of Detroit worked on the staff of the *Fifth Estate*. Both the independent newspapers and organs of political parties encouraged a relationship between reader and publisher that challenged the one-way transmission of news and information characteristic of the establishment press. Most staff members worked on a volunteer basis, and financially supported the papers, rather than the other way around, proving how vital publication was to the growing counterculture and how closely readers and newspapers could cooperate to meet social needs. These connections between expression and action looked dangerous to those who feared changes in the status quo. Community participation bent on alternative ways of doing things provoked suspicion. The government perceived in these grass roots relationships "anti-social" threats.

The new journalism, it seemed, was partly responsible for the increased political power of the hippies, New Left and anti-war movements. The government move against the underground press was clearly intended to blunt a potential force for political and social change. Official police agencies, however, rarely admitted they were prosecuting alternative papers for their political positions, but alleged that press offices were used as meeting places to plan illegal, even terrorist activities. They hunted for marijuana, arrested editors for obscenity,

Vol. 9, No 8, Issue 210, August 22-28, 1969
2042 University Ave., Berkeley, Ca. 94704 849-1040

PUBLISHED
WEEKLY   204

15¢ BAY AREA

25c ELSEWHERE

PARANOIA

and quibbled over street vending rights.

At the same time, most underground journals regarded the publication of erotic art, four-letter words, and discussions about drugs and alternative living to be acts of cultural enlightenment. They viewed arrests for drug violations, distribution of "pornographic" literature, and unlicensed vending as political arrests while government agencies worked to dissociate these forms of harassment from any notion of political repression. In fact, the government rarely attempted to prosecute any underground newspaper for its open political statements and *never obtained a conviction on a political charge*. Often the real issues of freedom of the press never came to light. Faced with the prospect of trials on petty charges, and unable to meet court costs, underground papers were ruined. Fourth Amendment rights were violated in searches and seizures of equipment by police agents. Records were lost, typewriters destroyed, and staffs disbanded as a result of police raids. When they failed to find drugs, agents nevertheless ransacked equipment and files. In other cases, where drugs were found, police brought publication to a halt by arresting an entire staff rather than charging an individual offender.

Neither the severity nor the scope of this outrageous campaign of harassment against alternative media was reported by major American news organizations. Equating partisanship with a failure to tell the truth, most establishment journalists did not see, in the move against vanguard and counterculture presses, a more general threat to constitutional guarantees of free expression and seldom looked behind the scenes to investigate harassment as a deliberate attempt to silence an adversary voice. There was no eagerness to cover an underground press that often vociferously criticized establishment media.

Most of the time, government interference with underground writing was reported in an uncoordinated and local manner. The sudden refusal of a printer to continue printing a paper[1], an overnight doubling of a journal's office rent,[2] advertising cancellations,[3] or shipping losses[4] fostered a not unjustified suspicion of large-scale interference by government agencies. Officials dismissed such complaints as "paranoid."

Given the bizarre nature of some of these cases, established media and even some sectors of the underground were inclined to agree.

The frequent failures of alternative newspapers and the many arrests of staff members were greeted in some quarters as an indication of the tenuous, "off the wall," and irresponsible nature of underground journalism. The failures and arrests bred an insecurity among staff members that itself contributed to the failure of several publications.

Now, however, the facts unearthed in the late 1970s by Congressional hearings, and documents the FBI was forced to release to those it spied on, tell a different story. They reveal how extensively government interference contributed to the failure of underground papers. When young people were politicized, when writers and intellectuals came out against the war, and when alternative journalism began to have political clout, intelligence agencies responded with a comprehensive program to put the lid on free expression. This meant surveillance, illegal covert action, intimidation, and harassment at federal, state, and local levels.

This report collates evidence gathered from defunct alternative publications and from those that survived despite continuing persecution. Important corroboration comes from Senate and House hearings on the U.S. intelligence agencies and from information made available through the Freedom of Information Act. It is the nature of the bureaucratic beast that its agencies' crimes often lie hidden for years, only made public years later, when it is politically expedient to do so. The events outlined in this report are not simply a matter of history—they are a warning for the future of free expression in this country.

THE NETWORK OF SUPPRESSION

ᵖᵉᵃᶜᵉ ᵃⁿᵈ ᶠʳᵉᵉᵈᵒᵐ ᵗʰʳᵘ ⁿᵒⁿ ᵛⁱᵒˡᵉⁿᵗ ᵃᶜᵗⁱᵒⁿ

WIN

March 1972   75¢

THE COMPLETE COLLECTION OF POLITICAL DOCUMENTS RIPPED-OFF FROM THE F.B.I. OFFICE IN MEDIA, PA., MARCH 8, 1971

WIN printed an entire FBI dossier detailing the
agency's sabotage of underground papers.

THE NETWORK OF SUPPRESSION

During the 1960s and 1970s, there was no unified government policy coordinating the control of writing and publishing. Manipulation and harassment were not part of a campaign orchestrated by a single administration and carried out through federal, state, and local law enforcement agencies. Rather, disparate operations met the demands of particular presidential administrations and were dependent upon the needs, interests, spheres of influence, and methods of the agencies themselves.

Although theoretically answerable to an elected authority, these agencies acted with relative autonomy. Because intelligence bureaucracies outlive presidential administrations, each agency is able to perpetuate itself by maintaining a cloud of secrecy around its operations to keep "outsiders" from full knowledge or control of its maneuvers.

SPYING TOGETHER

Every presidential administration, however, did try to control intelligence and law enforcement agencies through directives, suggestions, appointments, and, when police agents got out of hand, by censure. In the mid 1960s, Lyndon Johnson tried to engineer a coordinated system of investigation. After an administrative meeting on urban riots, the Federal Bureau of Investigation set up a Security Index and a Rabble Rouser Index.[5] Under Richard Nixon, these lists were expanded and made available to all federal agencies. In 1967, responding to pressure from the Johnson administration, the CIA and the National Security Agency joined forces in an enlarged domestic intelligence program to ferret out "foreign influences" on domestic unrest. Along with the FBI and CIA, the National Security Agency put together a "Watch List" of dissident Americans.[6] The Nixon administration profited from advances in technology and put computers and electronic tapes to work in the most powerful and extensive intelligence network ever seen in America.

While centralized intelligence information required cooperation among intelligence and law enforcement agencies, each agency fashioned its *own* program of domestic surveillance and grew inflated with ever bigger operations.

In 1970, the Nixon administration created the Interagency Committee on Intelligence, made up of the directors of the CIA, NSA, FBI, and the Defense Intelligence Agency. From its machinations, presidential advisor Tom Huston prepared the notorious Huston Plan—a domestic and foreign intelligence program to be controlled by the President. This plan called for opening mail, electronic surveillance, monitoring communications, break-ins, and campus infiltration.[7] It was partially implemented, bringing a new cohesiveness to Federal agencies. It did not prevent various agencies from acting on their own. For example, the National Security Agency had been monitoring domestic communications and the CIA had been opening citizens' mail for years without letting either the FBI or the Nixon administration know what they were doing.[8]

In fact, each agency cooperated with the President and police agencies only when that cooperation served its own interests. Usually, this meant *expansion* and *intensification* of that agency's authority. While the CIA and NSA were extending domestic surveillance, military intelligence began to monitor civilians as well as military personnel. At this time, the IRS used its tax intelligence division as a political weapon. The common link in this new net of spying was the local police, working with these federal agencies to increase their own power. Far from being a single, well-coordinated and planned offensive, then, the campaign against the underground press was executed by separate, often competing agencies. State and local law enforcement intelligence divisions, acting on their own initiative, launched investigations. While regional police often worked in tandem with federal agencies or through the Law Enforcement Intelligence Union (LEIU), they also paid attention to local political pressures. In monitoring and controlling underground writing, each police agency used its own strategy.

YOU'RE IN THE ARMY NOW

Armed Forces intelligence operated openly when dealing with outspoken military personnel, presuming the right to control those already subject to military authority. Throughout the early 1960s, military intelligence agents maintained a public profile, even when dealing with nonmilitary groups. But in 1967, when the Armed Forces intelligence program was augmented to hunt for threats of civil disorder[9], agents did surreptitious spying on both military personnel *and* on civilians. Of course, military intelligence openly scrutinized writing and publishing by military personnel.

In 1971, after Congress held hearings on domestic intelligence, the military was pressured to reduce its surveillance of civilians. The Department of Defense established a Defense Investigative Review Council (DIRC) to oversee military intelligence plans that targeted civilian groups. However, the DIRC approved many surveillance operations, including spying on a California underground newspaper, in 1971-1972.[10]

Because military intelligence maintained close ties with the FBI, it often acted as the FBI liaison abroad, insinuating agents into United States civilian and military groups. Between 1972 and 1975, Army and Navy intelligence closely monitored and attempted to infiltrate staffs of underground newspapers published by United States citizens in Japan and West Germany.[11] Among others were *Fight Back*, published in Heidelberg, and *Forward*, in West Berlin.

During the last twenty years, military intelligence has played an ominous role in the affairs of civilian writers at home as well. On January 14, 1969, Army intelligence took part in an FBI search of the offices of the *Free Press*, a Washington, D.C., underground newspaper. The Army agents kept the documents they found in the search. Throughout the 1960s, Army intelligence and the Chicago Police Department regularly exchanged intelligence information. When restrictions placed on military intelligence in 1971 called for destroying files on civilians, Army agents in Chicago, Cleveland, Pennsylvania, and Washington, D.C., gave the files instead to local and state police.[12]

FBI: DISRUPTING THE NEW LEFT

OPTIONAL FORM NO. 10
MAY 1962 EDITION
GSA GEN REG NO 27

UNITED STATES GOVERNMENT

Memorandum

TO : Mr. W. C. Sullivan

FROM : C. D. Brennan

SUBJECT : COUNTERINTELLIGENCE PROGRAM
INTERNAL SECURITY
DISRUPTION OF THE NEW LEFT
(COINTELPRO - NEW LEFT)

By letter dated 5/10/68 to all offices, the Bureau requested suggestions for counterintelligence action against the New Left. The replies to the Bureau's request have been analyzed. Many suggestions were made which were applicable to all offices.

These suggestions include preparation of a leaflet designed to counteract the impression that Students for a Democratic Society (SDS) and other minority groups speak for the majority of the students; the taking advantage of personal conflicts between New Left leaders; the creating of impressions that certain New Left leaders are informants; the use of articles from student and "underground" newspapers to show the depravity of New Left leaders and members; the preparation of anonymous letters to authorities and to parents of individuals active in the New Left setting out the activities of New Left members; anonymous letters to university officials protesting the actions of certain faculty members; the exploiting of hostility between New Left groups and such organizations as the Progressive Labor Party (PLP), a pro-Chinese, Marxist group; the use of ridicule against the New Left; and the pointing out and the calling attention to the use of narcotics by these individuals.

There is enclosed a letter to all offices setting out these suggestions. All offices are reminded that they are to take no counterintelligence action without Bureau approval.

EX 106

JUL 10 1968

RECOMMENDATION:

That the enclosed letter to all offices be approved.

Enclosure
100-449698
BAW:jes
(8)

1 - Mr. DeLoach
1 - Mr. Felt
1 - Mr. Bishop

1 - Mr. W.C. Sullivan
1 - Mr. C.D. Brennan
1 - Mr. Thompson
1 - Mr. D.A. Wells

Sent 7-8-68

COINTELPRO: THE "MORAL MINORITY"

The FBI worked well with military intelligence. They shared a highly authoritarian internal structure, and, during the 1960s, saw themselves as defenders of a rigorously structured society against the incursion of subversive elements.[13] The FBI, under J. Edgar Hoover, was an immensely powerful bureaucracy that made a public virtue of its secrecy. Until Hoover's death it was virtually free from Congressional oversight or executive review. In addition to implementing presidential initiatives, its independence enabled it to wield great power in the determination of policy.

In 1956, in the wake of the McCarthy era, the FBI initiated its vast counterintelligence program (COINTELPRO) "to disrupt, expose, discredit, and otherwise neutralize the United States Communist Party and related organizations."[14] Although the FBI had worked closely with other elements in the federal government in carrying out the witch hunts of the early 1950s, the subsequent discrediting and censure of McCarthy's activities made Hoover see the FBI as the last bastion in the war against "communist subversion" of the government. The Bureau surrounded its COINTELPRO operations with such secrecy that no President or advisor was ever aware of its entire scope.

Under COINTELPRO, the FBI planted stories about "subversives" in the media, wrote scurrilous letters from fictional sources, opened mail, forged public documents, pressured universities and employers to dismiss targeted workers, encouraged "friendly" organizations and local police to harass dissidents, exploited IRS tax records, and infiltrated legal organizations. Expanding well beyond harassment of Communist Party members, the FBI operation soon included any group with a left, socialist, pacifist, or minority rights position the agency arbitrarily judged "subversive."[15]

The FBI viewed underground writing in the 1960s and 1970s as one part of a concentrated political movement threatening the security of this country. The authority of COINTELPRO expanded to include the monitoring of putative "foreign infiltration" of newly-formed domestic political movements. No proof ever appeared that the underground press was under foreign influence, and the Church Report found that the FBI failed to provide a shred of evidence of it. As in so many other cases, this "infiltration" proved to be pure fiction. In fact, much of the vigor of the U.S. underground press arose from its indigenous spontaneity and cantankerous nature. At the same time, the FBI was able to exploit this rather uncoordinated obstreperousness for its own ends.

COINTELPRO was directed against New Left, anti-war and women's groups, Black Liberation and civil rights organizations, as well as individuals such as Martin Luther King, Jr. The way was opened for a full-scale FBI program against constitutionally guaranteed rights of free speech. The FBI interpreted a Presidential instruction from the 1950s as a mandate to disrupt by any means all political activity not in agreement with current official policy. Lists of "subversives" were drawn up, along with new definitions of threats to national security. This led the agency to participate in illegal break-ins as well as to create a new monitoring bureau—the Interdivisional Information Unity (IDIU)[16], a data bank of all information collected by a number of agencies.

THIS IS YOUR FBI

In an FBI COINTELPRO memorandum, written July 5, 1968, from the Director to the office in Albany, N.Y., a twelve-point program was prepared for dealing with the New Left. Part of that program included the manipulation of both established and underground media.[17]

On November 5, 1968, the day Richard Nixon was elected president, J. Edgar Hoover sent to FBI offices around the country a memo zeroing in on "New Left Movement Publications." He requested an immediate "detailed survey concerning New Left-type publications being printed and circulated in your territory on a regular basis." He additionally asked for information on each paper's publisher, printer, sources of funds, identity of editorial staff, subversive connections, and possible foreign ramifications.

FBI: THE 12-POINT MASTER PLAN

SAC, Albany

Director, FBI (100-449698)

1 - Mr. DeLoach
1 - Mr. Felt
7/5/68

1 - Mr. Bishop
1 - Mr. W.C. Sullivan
1 - Mr. C.D. Brennan
1 -
1 -

COUNTERINTELLIGENCE PROGRAM
INTERNAL SECURITY
DISRUPTION OF THE NEW LEFT
(COINTELPRO - NEW)LEFT)

  Bulet 5/10/68 requested suggestions for counterintelligence action against the New Left. The replies to
the Bureau's request have been analyzed and it is felt that
the following suggestions for counterintelligence action can
be utilized by all offices:

  1. Preparation of a leaflet designed to counteract the impression that Students for a Democratic Society
(SDS) and other minority groups speak for the majority of
students at universities. The leaflet should contain photographs of New Left leadership at the respective university.
Naturally, the most obnoxious pictures should be used.

  2. The instigating of or the taking advantage of
personal conflicts or animosities existing between New Left
leaders.

  3. The creating of impressions that certain New
Left leaders are informants for the Bureau or other law
enforcement agencies.

  4. The use of articles from student newspapers
and/or the "underground press" to show the depravity of
New Left leaders and members. In this connection, articles
showing advocation of the use of narcotics and free sex are
ideal to send to university officials, wealthy donors,
members of the legislature and parents of students who are
active in New Left matters.

  5. Since the use of marijuana and other narcotics
is widespread among members of the New Left, you should be
alert to opportunities to have them arrested by local
authorities on drug charges. Any information concerning the

2 - All Field Offices

BAW:jes
(12)

SEE NOTE PAGE THREE

Letter to SAC, Albany
RE: COUNTERINTELLIGENCE PROGRAM
100-449698

fact that individuals have marijuana or are engaging in a
narcotics party should be immediately furnished to local
authorities and they should be encouraged to take action.

      6. The drawing up of anonymous letters regarding
individuals active in the New Left. These letters should
set out their activities and should be sent to their parents,
neighbors and the parents' employers. This could have the
effect of forcing the parents to take action.

      7. Anonymous letters or leaflets describing
faculty members and graduate assistants in the various
institutions of higher learning who are active in New Left matters.
The activities and associations of the individual should be
set out. Anonymous mailings should be made to university
officials, members of the state legislature, Board of
Regents, and to the press. Such letters could be signed
"A Concerned Alumni" or "A Concerned Taxpayer."

      8. Whenever New Left groups engage in disruptive
activities on college campuses, cooperative press contacts
should be encouraged to emphasize that the disruptive
elements constitute a minority of the students and do not
represent the conviction of the majority. The press should
demand an immediate student referendum on the issue in
question. Inasmuch as the overwhelming majority of students
is not active in New Left matters, it is felt that this
technique, used in carefully selected cases, could put an
end to lengthy demonstrations and could cause embarrassment
to New Left elements.

      9. There is a definite hostility among SDS and
other New Left groups toward the Socialist Workers Party
(SWP), the Young Socialist Alliance (YSA), and the
Progressive Labor Party (PLP). This hostility should be
exploited wherever possible.

      10. The field was previously advised that New Left
groups are attempting to open coffeehouses near military
bases in order to influence members of the Armed Forces.
Wherever these coffeehouses are, friendly news media should
be alerted to them and their purpose. In addition, various

Letter to SAC, Albany
RE: COUNTERINTELLIGENCE PROGRAM
100-449698

drugs, such as marijuana, will probably be utilized by
individuals running the coffeehouses or frequenting them.
Local law enforcement authorities should be promptly advised
whenever you receive an indication that this is being done.

        11. Consider the use of cartoons, photographs, and
anonymous letters which will have the effect of ridiculing
the New Left. Ridicule is one of the most potent weapons
which we can use against it.

        12. Be alert for opportunities to confuse and
disrupt New Left activities by misinformation. For example,
when events are planned, notification that the event has
been cancelled or postponed could be sent to various
individuals.

        You are reminded that no counterintelligence
action is to be taken without Bureau approval. Insure that
this Program is assigned to an Agent with an excellent
knowledge of both New Left groups and individuals. It must
be approached with imagination and enthusiasm if it is to be
successful.

        As an economy measure the caption "COINTELPRO - NEW LEFT"
should be used on all communications concerning this Program.

NOTE:

        See memo C.D. Brennan to W.C. Sullivan dated
7/3/68, captioned as above, prepared by BAW: jes.

- 3 -

FBI: DUPLICITY AND DEVIOUS MANEUVERS

SAC, Albany   August 25, 1967

                                        PERSONAL ATTENTION TO ALL OFFICES

Director, FBI
                                                    1 - Mr. C.D. Brennan
                                                    1 -
COUNTERINTELLIGENCE PROGRAM   1 -
BLACK NATIONALIST - HATE GROUPS   1 -
INTERNAL SECURITY   1 -
                                                    1 -

          Offices receiving copies of this letter are instructed
to immediately establish a control file, captioned as above, and
to assign responsibility for following and coordinating this new
counterintelligence program to an experienced and imaginative
Special Agent well versed in investigations relating to black
nationalist, hate-type organizations. The field office control
file used under this program may be maintained in a pending
inactive status until such time as a specific operation or
technique is placed under consideration for implementation.

          The purpose of this new counterintelligence endeavor
is to expose, disrupt, misdirect, discredit, or otherwise
neutralize the activities of black nationalist, hate-type
organizations and groupings, their leadership, spokesmen,
membership, and supporters, and to counter their propensity for
violence and civil disorder. The activities of all such groups
of intelligence interest to this Bureau must be followed on a
continuous basis so we will be in a position to promptly take
advantage of all opportunities for counterintelligence and to
inspire action in instances where circumstances warrant. The
pernicious background of such groups, their duplicity, and devious
maneuvers must be exposed to public scrutiny where such publicity
will have a neutralizing effect. Efforts of the various groups,

MCT-34   100-   448006

REC 34

2 - Atlanta   2 - Philadelphia
2 - Baltimore   2 - Phoenix
2 - Boston   2 - Pittsburgh
2 - Buffalo   2 - Richmond   18 AUG 2
2 - Charlotte   X 100   2 - St. Louis
2 - Chicago   2 - San Francisco
2 - Cincinnati   2 - Washington Field Office
2 - Cleveland
2 - Detroit
2 - Jackson
2 - Los Angeles
3 - Memphis
2 - Newark
2 - New Orleans
2 - New York

ALL INFORMATION CONTAINED
HEREIN IS UNCLASSIFIED
EXCEPT WHERE SHOWN
OTHERWISE.

MAIL ROOM □   TELETYPE UNIT □

Letter to SAC, Albany
RE: COUNTERINTELLIGENCE PROGRAM
     BLACK NATIONALIST - HATE GROUPS

to consolidate their forces or to recruit new or youthful
adherents must be frustrated. No opportunity should be missed
to exploit through counterintelligence techniques the
organizational and personal conflicts of the leaderships of the
groups and where possible an effort should be made to capitalize
upon existing conflicts between competing black nationalist
organizations. When an opportunity is apparent to disrupt or
neutralize black nationalist, hate-type organizations through the
cooperation of established local news media contacts or through
such contact with sources available to the Seat of Government,
in every instance careful attention must be given to the proposal
to insure the targeted group is disrupted, ridiculed, or
discredited through the publicity and not merely publicized.
Consideration should be given to techniques to preclude violence-
prone or rabble-rouser leaders of hate groups from spreading their
philosophy publicly or through various mass communication media.

          Many individuals currently active in black nationalist
organizations have backgrounds of immorality, subversive activity,
and criminal records. Through your investigation of key agitators
you should endeavor to establish their unsavory backgrounds.
Be alert to determine evidence of misappropriation of funds or
other types of personal misconduct on the part of militant
nationalist leaders so any practical or warranted counterintelligence may be instituted.

          Intensified attention under this program should be
afforded to the activities of such groups as the Student
Nonviolent Coordinating Committee, the Southern Christian
Leadership Conference, Revolutionary Action Movement, the
Deacons for Defense and Justice, Congress of Racial Equality,
and the Nation of Islam. Particular emphasis should be given to
extremists who direct the activities and policies of
revolutionary or militant groups such as Stokely Carmichael,
H. "Rap" Brown, Elijah Muhammad, and Maxwell Stanford.

          At this time the Bureau is setting up no requirement
for status letters to be periodically submitted under this
program. It will be incumbent upon you to insure the program
is being afforded necessary and continuing attention and that
no opportunities will be overlooked for counterintelligence
action.

          This program should not be confused with the program
entitled "Communist Party, USA, Counterintelligence Program,
Internal Security - C," (Bufile 100-3-104), which is directed

-2-

Letter to SAC, Albany
RE: COUNTERINTELLIGENCE PROGRAM
      BLACK NATIONALIST - HATE GROUPS

against the Communist Party and related organizations, or the
program entitled "Counterintelligence Program, Internal Security,
Disruption of Hate Groups," (Bufile 157-9), which is directed
against Klan and hate-type groups primarily consisting of white
memberships.

        All Special Agent personnel responsible for the
investigation of black nationalist, hate-type organizations and
their memberships should be alerted to our counterintelligence
interest and each Investigative Agent has a responsibility to
call to the attention of the counterintelligence coordinator
suggestions and possibilities for implementing the program.
You are also cautioned that the nature of this new endeavor
is such that under no circumstances should the existence of
the program be made known outside the Bureau and appropriate
within-office security should be afforded to sensitive operations
and techniques considered under the program.

        No counterintelligence action under this program may
be initiated by the field without specific prior Bureau
authorization.

        You are urged to take an enthusiastic and imaginative
approach to this new counterintelligence endeavor and the Bureau
will be pleased to entertain any suggestions or techniques you
may recommend.

FBI: MONITORING PHONE CALLS AND BANK ACCOUNTS

The New Jersey Telephone Co. Directory for March, 1967, lists telephone number 638-6872 to David Dellinger, R.D. Hampton, N.J. The New Jersey Telephone Co. Directory for March, 1968, includes no listing for DAVID DELLINGER or any other DELLINGER. On 6/3/68, Mr. ███████████████████ was contacted by SA ██████████████ to determine whether DAVID DELLINGER still had a telephone. At the mention of DAVID DELLINGER's name, Mr. ████████ expressed indignation at DELLINGER's pacifist activities, gratification that his activities were not being overlooked, and admiration for the effective work of the FBI. He volunteered the following information most eagerly; but on a confidential basis:...(Listing of telephone calls made)·

... It is plan of the Newark Office to again review the bank account of ████████ as well as the toll charges to the telephone at the DELLINGER residence. Contact will be maintained with ████████ and with Post Office personnel at both Glen Gardner and Hampton, N.J....

While it is a fact that DELLINGER has a residence in Hampton, N.J., it is also a fact that his activities in which the Bureau has an interest, are based in New York, for example, Liberation Magazine, National Mobilization Committee to End the War in Vietnam, and the Fifth Avenue Vietnam Peace Parade Committee. Further, the bank accounts for these organizations, in which DELLINGER holds officership, are located in New York City. In addition, ████████ advised on 4/16/68. that DAVID DELLINGER stays with various friends while in New York City. Since the subject is, in effect spending the major portion of his time in New York, it is recommended by Newark that the New York Office be made Office of Origin in this matter.

A recommendation for inclusion of DAVID DELLINGER on the Agitator Index is going forward by separate communication.

Excerpts from FBI Document #HK 100-41323

FBI: ATTACHING THE STIGMA OF "FINK"

NK 100-50156

own destruction. Each field office should acquire the names and backgrounds of all students of the "new left", who have been arrested for the very type of activity we are now trying to curtail or halt. Any Government subsidization to these individuals should be stopped.

They must be taken out of the ranks of this pre-dominantly college-age movement; separate them and diminish their power.

2. Certain key leaders must be chosen to become the object of a counterintelligence plot to identify them as government informants. It appears that this is the only thing that could cause these individuals concern; if some of their leaders turned out to be paid informers. Attacking their morals, disrespect for the law, or patriotic disdain will not impress their followers, as it would normally to other groups, so it must be by attacking them through their own principles and beliefs. Accuse them of selling out to "imperialistic monopoly capitalism".

THOMAS EMMETT HAYDEN
KEY ACTIVIST, NEWARK DIVISION

Newark believes that it might be possible to attach the stigma of informant or Government "fink" to HAYDEN because of the apparent unlimited finances at his disposal, enabling him to take numerous trips in and out of the U.S., without any job or other means of financial support. Also, the ease with which he travels to communist countries, his reception there, the privileges afforded him, and his eventual return with no actual remonstrations by this Government.

Newark suggests that after HAYDEN visits a certain city or country, that a news release, datelined Washington, D.C., be prepared noting that "according to informed Government sources", etc., certain events happened in that certain city or country which would reflect back on HAYDEN through similarity of circumstances or events. It is suggested further that these news releases be collected and when several promis-ing items are collected, they be turned over to a representative of a cooperative news media with a suggestion that a feature

NK 100-30106

writer be given the task of writing up a story pointing out
the coincidences of HAYDEN's visits to certain cities and
news stories emanating from Washington, D.C., pointing to
HAYDEN as the source. The connection may be spotlighted by
including certain sidelights or confidential bits of information which may only be known to HAYDEN and a Bureau source.

It is realized the above will take time, but in
order for the plan to be effective, it must have a solid
basis and a continual indictment.

One copy of this letter is being sent to Chicago
since THOMAS HAYDEN changed his residence to there.

One copy of this letter is being sent to NYO for
information because of available transportation facilities
which give "new left" demonstrators in this area the opportunity to choose either New York or New Jersey locations
for disruptive tactics.

FBI: EXPLOITING FRIENDLY MEDIA

UNITED STATES GOVERNMENT

Memorandum

TO : Mr. W. C. Sullivan   DATE: May 22, 1968

FROM : C. D. Brennan

SUBJECT: COUNTERINTELLIGENCE PROGRAM
INTERNAL SECURITY
DISRUPTION OF THE NEW LEFT

You will recall that the Director approved my
memorandum of May 9, 1968, setting up a Counterintelligence
Program, and a letter was directed to all offices on May 10,
1968, requesting an analysis and recommendations on potential
action to be instituted against New Left organizations and Key
Activists. This information is to reach the Bureau on or
before June 1, 1968, and it is expected to provide a broad
analysis whereby specific areas of concentration can be
selected for a counterintelligence operation.

In the meantime, it is felt there are several areas
where data in possession of field offices should be immediately
solicited in depth so that prompt assimilation and dissemination
to the news media can be instituted to discredit the New Left
movement and its adherents. In this regard, a proposed letter
to all offices is attached requesting detailed information on
false allegations of police brutality and/or violence used
on police, immorality, and action taken by college administrators when confronted by student disorders. It is anticipated
this information can be used through friendly news media to
vividly portray the revolutionary-type actions and militant
nature of the New Left movement, as well as to show that firm
action by college officials has been successful in dealing
with insurgents.

RECOMMENDATION:

That the attached letter be sent to all offices.

Enclosure

1 - Mr. C.D. DeLoach
1 - Mr. W.C. Sullivan
1 - Mr. C.D. Brennan
1 -
1 -
RLR:sib
   (6)

FBI: WRITING EXTREMELY RADICAL ON THEIR FACE

```
                        U                    1 - Mr. DeLoach
                                             1 - Mr. W.C. Sullivan
                                             1 - Mr. C.D. Brennan
     SAC, Albany                                   5/29/68

                                             1 - ▓▓▓▓▓▓▓▓▓▓
     Director, FBI (100-449698)              1 - ▓▓▓▓▓▓▓▓▓▓

     COUNTERINTELLIGENCE PROGRAM
     INTERNAL SECURITY
     DISRUPTION OF THE NEW LEFT


              In connection with your review of college campus
     newspapers, you should commence submitting articles which
     might be utilized for appropriate dissemination.  Items submitted
     should be extremely radical on their face, use profanity
     or be repulsive in nature.  It is anticipated these
     articles, editorials, letters to the editor, et cetera, can
     be effectively utilized through dissemination to responsible
     individuals, such as state legislators, friendly news media
     and the like.

              Articles submitted should be appropriately mounted
     and accompanied by an unclipped copy of the same newspaper
     in which it appeared.  Your recommendations for dissemination
     outlets should accompany each article.
```

FBI memoranda of 10/11/68 and 1/17/79 document the Bureau's creation of two mock underground publications, *Armageddon News* in Indiana and *Longhorn Tales* in Texas, to promote the view that most students were not participating in protest movements.[18] The FBI believed that one of its best weapons against the New Left was the "shocking" writing and art in underground publications. The agency found ideas about sexual and political liberation in these journals to be decadent and depraved. The moral indignation the Bureau expressed in COINTELPRO memoranda was used to rationalize and exercise unmandated powers against independent publications. The older crusade against "Communist" influence became a crusade against the emerging counterculture. The campaign against alien subversion became a campaign against dissent and alternative strategies for living.

CIA: POLITICAL ILLEGALITY: OPERATION CHAOS

The Central Intelligence Agency, on the other hand, did not rely on a moralistic position to justify action against underground writing and the counterculture. Instead it saw itself as a highly professional agency whose purpose was to carry out, overtly and covertly, the wishes of the executive branch. Yet CIA agents soon took on powers that were often illegal and unknown to those they served. The CIA's domestic mail-opening program, which ran from 1952 through 1973, was hidden from Presidents Truman, Eisenhower, Kennedy, and possibly Johnson. So secret were these machinations that not only was the Postmaster General kept in the dark, but even CIA directors John McCone and Admiral William F. Raborn, Jr. claimed ignorance.[19]

While the CIA had originally been created for foreign intelligence operations, it became more and more occupied with dissident activity at home. The Counter-Intelligence Division of the CIA initiated Operation Chaos at the behest of the Johnson administration in 1967 to determine foreign influence on antiwar groups.[20] The CIA interpreted this request as a license to conduct illegal surveillance and disruption.

In general CIA agents had a more liberal outlook than those in the FBI. This was particularly true in the early years when the agency was evolving out of the World War II Office of Strategic Services (OSS). Even though the "dirty tricks" of the Counter-Intelligence branch began to dominate operations, the agency still regarded its effort as a skilled professional campaign against a political enemy in which questions of public morals or legality were irrelevant. Thus it did not, like the FBI, become histrionic over sex and drugs in the underground. The CIA's public rationale was that the counterculture and its publications were giving comfort and support to the North Vietnamese and the Viet Cong, and that, therefore, its actions against them were a domestic front in the Vietnam war effort.

A substantial percentage of CIA recruits came from patrician families, graduated from Ivy League universities and were connected with business, legal, and financial powers.[21]

This accounts for the high level of analysis and the tone of *noblesse oblige* in agency reports. The "Situation Information Report: The Underground Press" (April 26, 1973) found that:

> "The underground press, an inaccurate name used mostly for its romantic connotations, was the product of a changing national consciousness reflected most visibly by young people . . . Although lacking a clear analysis of current events, many of the new underground—and the old ones that didn't fold up in the transitional stage—made motions to Marxism but actually leaned heavily toward anarchism. . . . The 1969 SDS national convention, which split SDS into a number of opposing factions, signalled the downfall of the underground press. Lacking national focus and leadership, each paper was forced to define its role and develop its own political line based on what remained of the radical youth movement, its own readership and financial backers. Most papers vacillated during the ensuing months and many more folded in the process.
>
> The underground press is now in decline. It would appear that the vitality of the "alternative" press was directly proportional to the health of the radical movement in general. The underground press arose from the ferment of the times and the abatement of that ferment has undercut its strength and need."

While this document is an astute assessment of the decline of the underground press, it is also an example of how the agency left part of the story untold—that part which documents the culpability of federal agencies. The CIA devised special programs, with code names like Operation Chaos and project Resistance, to move against all segments of the counterculture, not only the underground press. Its agents shadowed writers by exchanging information with the FBI, NSA, IRA and local police forces. It trained local and state agents in spying techniques and offered them surveillance equipment.[22] While subsidizing intellectual organs, such as the Congress for Cultural Freedom, it unlawfully invaded the lives of writers and editors. With the backing of Presidents Johnson and Nixon, it undertook secret, illegal action against literary dissidents.

There are ironies in the CIA story. James Angleton, head of the Counter-Intelligence Division had edited a literary magazine, *Furioso*, after he graduated from Yale, and he maintained ties of a decidedly dissident, albeit not left wing, character, such as his friendship with Ezra Pound. And the CIA carried out programs of drug experimentation (the agency's role in Southeast Asian heroin trafficking is now public knowledge). As John Marks's *The Search for the Manchurian Candidate* points out, the CIA initiated some of the first experiments which tested the influence of psychedelic drugs on writing.[23] The CIA was more sophisticated than the FBI. It went in for infiltrating news staffs, whereas the FBI toyed with the idea of spraying newspapers with foul odors. Still, it was no less militant in its action to suppress free speech.

Cartoon by Miller in the G.I. paper *Forward, 1974*

WATCH LISTS AND RED SQUADS

The CIA, FBI, and military intelligence were not the only conspirators in the manipulation of underground writing. The Special Services Staff and the Intelligence Division of the Internal Revenue Service used their powers to audit tax returns and collect confidential information to harass and spy on allegedly dangerous writers. The Special Services Staff Director, for example, asked the Detroit District Office of the IRS to investigate the Radical Education Project as part of the IRS's participation in "an effort to save the country from dissidents and extremists."[24] At the request of the CIA, the IRS audited Victor Marchetti in 1972, while he was writing a critique of the CIA. It investigated *Ramparts* magazine in 1967, following its publication of an article detailing CIA connections with the National Student Association.[25] Not only useful to the CIA, the IRS also served the Nixon administration as an instrument to stifle dissent. In a 1970 memorandum, a Nixon aide stated: "What we cannot do in a court room via criminal prosecutions to curtail the activities of some of these groups, IRS could do by administrative action."[26]

The National Security Agency, with a high-tech electronic spying apparatus and a "watch list" (compiled with the help of the CIA, FBI, Secret Service, and the Bureau of Narcotics and Dangerous Drugs[27]) had the power to monitor the communications of over 75,000 Americans. The data they gathered illegally went into a vast information storage system, for purposes of future control of free speech.

In 1956, local and state police formed their own intelligence network, the Law Enforcement Intelligence Unit (LEIU), independent of federal control. The LEIU hounded groups and individuals it branded "terrorist." A computerized Interstate Organized Crime Index was established by the LEIU to provide a central data bank for the program. In addition to supplying surveillance equipment, the CIA trained the LEIU's intelligence units, or Red Squads, in covert intelligence techniques, maintaining a liaison with the LEIU through the Fairfax County, Virginia, Police Department.[28] The FBI worked hand in glove with most police departments. Through them, it helped create several paramilitary vigilante groups that engaged in violent attacks on underground publishers. In addition, the 113th Military Intelligence Group provided money and arms for the Chicago Red Squad, which in turn passed the money along to a paramilitary organization, the Legion of Justice. The Legion became known for its vicious assaults on people who worked at underground papers and bookstores, on New Left activists, as well as for its theft of legal files belonging to the Chicago Conspiracy Trial lawyers. This Law Enforcement Intelligence Unit operated almost entirely in secret, with no regulation of its criteria for surveillance, its methods or its use of information.[29]

Many covert and illegal activities were encouraged by Presidents Johnson and Nixon, whose administration pushed for an unprecedented control over its critics. In addition to coordinating federal law enforcement and intelligence agencies, the Nixon administration moved to exploit the subpoena power of grand juries. The First Amendment rights of underground writing as free political and artistic expression were ignored.

While alternative media were only one aspect of a general social, political, and cultural movement, their importance to a pluralistic counterculture was not lost on entrenched interests. In time, the network of government control was to touch every writer, editor, publisher, printer, and distributor of underground writing. A coast-to-coast juggernaut was mobilized to keep tabs on every American who could be labeled "extremist," "communist," "socialist," "dissident," or sometimes even "liberal." Most small, independent underground publications could not withstand the pressures applied by the various agents of government.

A HISTORY OF HARASSMENT

NOLA EXPRESS

20¢

NEW ORLEANS Dec 19, '69 – Jan 1, 1970 / No. 45 / Second Class Postage Paid at New Orleans LA / 20¢ New Orleans / 25¢ National

REWARD

FOR INFORMATION LEADING TO THE APPREHENSION OF —

JESUS CHRIST

WANTED — FOR SEDITION, CRIMINAL A IARCHY-
VAGRANCY, ANI CONSPIRING TO OVERTI LOW THE
ESTABLISHED GOVERNMENT

DRESSES POORLY. SAID TO BE A CARPENTER BY TRADE, ILL —
NOURISHED, HAS VISIONARY IDEAS, ASSOCIATES WITH COMMON
WORKING PEOPLE THE UNEMPLOYED AND BUMS. ALIEN —
BELEIVED TO BE A JEW   ALIAS: 'PRINCE OF PEACE, SON OF
MAN' - 'LIGHT OF THE WORLD' &c &c   PROFESSIONAL AGITATOR
RED BEARD, MARKS ON HANDS AND FEET THE RESULT OF
INJURIES INFLICTED BY AN ANGRY MOB. LED BY RESPECTABLE
CITIZENS AND LEGAL AUTHORITIES.

Art Young

A HISTORY OF HARASSMENT

While Federal agencies were interfering with underground writing as one part of a large-scale offensive against progressive political movements, regional authorities, sometimes abetted by the FBI, disrupted community-centered alternative journals, seeing in them dangerous seeds of radical change.

Outside of large cities, underground publications were often the sole source of avant-garde literature, progressive news, and political information. Massive anti-war demonstrations, college campus unrest, experimentation with foreign religions and drugs, and an attitude of contempt for conventional national goals provoked a kind of hysterical reaction in many communities. At the same time, the alternative media took moral stands against war, violence, imperialism, racism, and the nuclear menace. Exuberant and provocative, it engaged in a kind of muckraking of business and political corruption — in the tradition of Lincoln Steffens, Ida Tarbell, and Upton Sinclair. The appalling horrors of the Vietnam War inspired scathing political invective. Many papers made liberal use of ribald satire and profanity. Others extolled drug use, sexual liberty, and theatrical politics in ways that were objectionable not only to conservatives, but also to some people in the Movement. To local authorities, underground newspapers seemed to be the focal points for an emerging social revolution that had to be stopped.

According to the Underground Press Syndicate, there were, in 1971, over 400 underground publications in this country.[30] By 1978, there were only 65, and more than a third of these had been founded after 1973.[31] This extraordinary rate of attrition was largely due to the pitched battle for survival these journals were forced to fight. The UPS reported that sixty per cent of its members had experienced a great deal of government interference,[32] ranging from distribution interruption, customer and printer harassment, to wiretaps, legal costs, infiltration by agents, and even bombings and bomb threats.

By using narcotics and obscenity statutes as a pretext, police found it easy to attack the new media on grounds which reflected a traditional, puritanical morality distinct from any notion of political rights. This strategy of oblique attack made an effective, if meretricious, appeal to people already uneasy about growing family and community instability, not to speak of terrifying developments in world affairs. While the thrust of much underground writing was to demonstrate the inextricable links between moral and political notions, government agencies sought to efface these larger issues with the imposition of arrests on phony charges and the sheer expense of legal fees, which effectively silenced many papers not cowed by physical abuse.

STREET CORNER JUSTICE

Preventing distribution was an effective disruption tactic. For the most part, underground papers were sold on the street. By exploiting the vague wording of vagrancy and pornography laws, the police frequently rounded up street vendors. After *The San Diego Free Press* published an investigative report in 1969 exposing a corrupt local businessman, the paper's street sellers were arrested at the rate of two a week. A single round-up brought in twenty-five vendors at one time.[33] In most cases, charges against vendors arrested for loitering were subsequently dismissed. This kind of tactic dissipated staff energy, made it difficult to recruit vendors, and meant lost revenues for the papers. Political activists became wary of selling papers on the street because arrests took time and money away from other projects. The editors of Spokane's *Natural* were arrested on vagrancy charges while trying to sell their paper. In New Orleans, people selling *NOLA Express* were arrested many times, in one case for "carrying a dangerous weapon"—the seller's umbrella. FBI intent to stop distribution of the *Black Panther Party Paper* surfaced in a COINTELPRO memorandum sent by the Newark office to J. Edgar Hoover, proposing that newspapers be sprayed with Skatole, a foul-smelling chemical. The Detroit office sent a similar request to the Director for "a solution capable of duplicating the scent of the most foul-smelling feces available . . . along with a dispenser capable of squirting a narrow stream for a distance of approximately three feet . . ." A flurry of memoranda followed, but the idea was never acted on.

FBI: SPRAYING PAPERS WITH FOUL ODORS

Date: 5/?/70

Transmit the following in _____
(Type in plaintext or code)

Via _____ AIRTEL _____
(Priority)

TO: DIRECTOR, FBI

FROM: SAC, NEWARK (100-49194) (P)

SUBJECT: COUNTERINTELLIGENCE PROGRAM
         BLACK PANTHER PARTY (BPP)
         RACIAL MATTERS

         Re Bureau airtel, 5/15/70.

         Newark submits the following as possible
measure to hinder distribution and effect of BPP
newspaper.

         In the light of known BPP procedures at
San Francisco re handling and bundling of the paper
prior to shipment to local chapters, an opportunity
might arise to spray the papers with a chemical known
as Skatole, ($C_9 H_9 N$). A very small amount of this
chemical disburses a most offensive odor on the object
sprayed and its potency is such that a large amount of
papers could be so treated in a matter of seconds.
It could be prepared by the FBI Laboratory for use in
an aerosol type dispenser.

         It is believed that this measure was previously
considered as a move to affect distribution of "The
Worker," but it is Newark's understanding that it was
considered inadvisable at that time. Inasmuch as Newark
does not have specific information re reasons its use
was not approved, it is suggested the Bureau review
previous use against "The Worker" for background in
this matter.

REC-34   100- 448006- 1901X1

② Bureau
1- San Francisco (INFO)
3- Newark
   (1- S2 Desk)
JWB/pds
(6)   EX-115   JUN 4 1970

JUL 22 1970

Approved: _____ Special Agent in Charge   Sent _____ M   Per _____

5-5 JUN 22 1970   65A

ALL INFORMATION CONTAINED
HEREIN IS UNCLASSIFIED
EXCEPT WHERE SHOWN
OTHERWISE

RACIAL INT SECT

The FBI often used intimidation against distributors as well as journals: simple persuasion worked from time to time, as when the FBI convinced a New York shipper for the *Black Panther Party Paper* to make his rates prohibitive.[35] After a visit by FBI agents, the distributor of the New York-based *Rat* refused to continue doing business with the paper.[36] In their vendetta against *Rat*, the FBI, according to a postal worker, ran a "cover" on the paper's mail, spying on all correspondence the editorial board received. The FBI documents also reveal that the Bureau owned subscription lists of the *East Village Other* and the *Yipster Times* and interviewed many of the subscribers.[37]

When twelve vendors from *NOLA Express* in New Orleans were arrested in a three-month period in 1969, the editors obtained an injunction against further arrests. The paper was banned from college campuses in the area. College authorities across the country banned the campus distribution of much underground journalism: in both Austin, Texas, and Madison, Wisconsin, papers like *The Rag* and *Kaleidoscope* were forbidden on campus. It took a three-judge federal panel to find this ban unconstitutional, ruling, "First Amendment freedoms are not dependent upon the will of an administrator."[38]

LOVE NOT WAR

Obscenity laws gave the police a tool that appealed to citizens disturbed by turbulent changes in the sexual mores of a large youthful population. While underground papers were describing napalming, bombing and defoliation in Vietnam and Cambodia as government-sponsored obscenities, police agents were prosecuting alternative journalists for printing four-letter words, "lewd" pictures, or depicting people making love. When the underground press transgressed conventional ideas of public decency, the government exploited the possibilities of clouding the issue of free expression.

Miami, Florida, was the scene of a nefarious campaign against *The Daily Planet*. Its editor was arrested twenty-nine times in 1969 and 1970 for selling obscene literature on the streets. Although he was acquitted twenty-eight times, he still had to pay nearly $93,000 in bail bonds.[39] When Allen Ginsberg came to Miami to give a benefit reading for *The Daily Planet*, the police broke up his reading of "Pentagon Exorcism." It took an appeal to the federal courts to prove that the reading was, in fact, constitutionally protected. The court ordered city officials to give *The Daily Planet* the municipal auditorium to complete the interrupted reading of his poem.

In March, 1969, *Open City* in Los Angeles was forced to pay court costs and a $1,000 fine on an obscenity conviction.[40] This paper was later vindicated by a higher court, but the punitive defense fees forced *Open City* out of business. The street vendors of *Kaleidoscope* in Madison, Wisconsin, were repeatedly arrested for selling obscene literature to minors.[41] As reported in the *New York Times*, this was only part of a campaign that included the publisher's arrest for obscenity, an editor's arrest for refusing to reveal sources, and the fire-bombing of the offices of the paper and an editor's car.

After one newsstand in New York City was fined for selling the *East Village Other*, which allegedly contained obscenity, other newsstands and bookstores were afraid to carry the paper.[42] After the newspaper had successfully won state and local obscenity cases in federal court, an entire printing of *Great Speckled Bird* of Atlanta was seized by the U.S. Postal Service in 1972 for printing abortion referral information. The same abortion advertisements had appeared in the *New York Times*. In one case, authorities had prosecuted *Great Speckled Bird* under an Atlanta city ordinance prohibiting the "use of any derogatory words relating to the methods of sexual intercourse with relatives or strangers."[43]

FBI: REFERRING TO INCEST, SEXUALITY AND BIOLOGY

OPTIONAL FORM NO. 10
MAY 1962 EDITION
GSA FPMR (41 CFR) 101-11.6

UNITED STATES GOVERNMENT

Memorandum

TO : DIRECTOR, FBI (100-449698)   DATE: 5/23/69

FROM : SAC, NEWARK (100-50166)(P)

SUBJECT: COINTELPRO-NEW LEFT

Re Newark letters 2/19, 4/1/69.

There are enclosed for the Bureau's perusal an issue of a newspaper published in NYC called "SCREW" dated 2/7/69 containing a type of filth that could only originate in a depraved mind.

It is representative of the type of mentality that is following the New Left theory of immorality on certain college campuses. Officials at Rutgers are, at the very least, condoning its distribution since no curtailment of its sale or distribution has been imposed by them. This paper is being given away and sold inside Conklin Hall, Rutgers University, Newark by "hippie" types in unkempt clothes, with wild beards, shoulder length hair and other examples of their non-conformity.

Newark proposes that this paper be sent to Senator WILLIAM T. HIERING, in the NJ Legislature.

It is suggested also that the following letter, typewritten on general "5x10" stationary be sent with the paper and mailed at Newark in vicinity of Rutgers campus:

"Dear Sir:

"I am a student at Rutgers Newark with a deep desire to educate myself and make for myself and my family, a place of respect in our great country.

I believe however that we are appoaching an era where the bad elements will outweigh the good. I am appalled at what is condoned by officials here at Newark Rutgers. I enclose an example of what is sold and freely distributed inside Conklin Hall, Rutgers, Newark. Would you want your children or grandchildren, especially young girls, subjected to such depravity? The question is of course rhetorical, no decent person would. But this is becoming a way of campus life. Poison the minds of the young, destroy their moral being and in less than one generation this country will be ripe for its downfall.

ENCLOSURE
REC-128

2-Bureau (enc. 1, OBSCENE)(RM)
1-Newark
DDO/ml
(3)   25 MAY 25 1969

Buy U.S. Savings Bonds Regularly on the Payroll Savings Plan

NK 100-50166

"One can say, these slime are in the minority but all
countries that were once great, but don't exist now,
contained that first minority (Ancient Rome and Greece for
example-Socrates warned them and now they and their
culture are gone.)

Safely assuming these papers represent an evil
force and it is distributed by a minority on campus, then
why do the moral majority have to put up with it. Rutgers
is supported by public funds and as a representative of the
people, you and your colleagues should have the courage to
take the initiative now to see that people like Mason Gross
do not misuse or misdirect those funds by condoning such
activity in the name of "academic freedom" and "free speech
and free press."

What irony if the money the people of New Jersey
voted for public education was instrumental in toppling their
own society.

You should exhibit this filth on the Senate floor
for your colleagues to see and it should also be brought to
the attention of the Joint Legislative Education Committee.

It surpasses greatly the experimental literature
distributed to the English classes at Paterson State College.

A Concerned Student"

Bureau requested to return enclosure with its
comments.

The experimental literature referred to in the
letter is a mimeographed copy, run off by Paterson State
College on their machine, of a short story titled "Tea Party"
published in "Evergreen Review". It was distributed by professors of literature to students in composition classes, at
Paterson State College. It contained 79 obscene terms
referring to incest, sexuality and biology, four dozen "cuss"
words and a dozen instances of taking the Lord's name in vain.

The NJ Senate as a result ordered an investigation
by the Senate Education Committee, headed by Senator WILLIAM
T. HIERING of Ocean County.

Newark believes an opportunity now exists to focus
lawmakers attention on the depraved nature of the type of
student now infesting campus activities as exemplified by
New Left adherents.

MEAT by Jack Minnis p.4

NOLA EXPRESS

NEW ORLEANS, LOUISIANA, Number 129, April 13 - 26, 1973, Second Class Postage Paid, 35¢ or barter.

© 1973 Psychedelic Art Foundation

SIX NUCLEAR FISSION POWER PLANTS PLANNED FOR LA.

There are six nuclear power plants being considered for siting in the region of Louisiana, including Waterford, Riverbend, a 900 MW (e) Boiling Water Reactor near St. Francisville, another Gulf States Utilities nuclear power plant planned near St. Francisville, a third Gulf States Utilities nuclear power plant in Texas on the Sabine River, and two nuclear plants of Mississippi Power and Light below Vicksburg.

- Will Pozzi
Research Investigator
Council on Environmental
Issues
LSU, Baton Rouge
Student Government Assoc.

NOLA EXPRESS: A PYRRHIC VICTORY

Generally, alternative presses won legal battles against government agencies. However, it often took years for judgments to be handed down, and the expenses of appealing often meant that the newspaper couldn't survive, even if it won its case. *NOLA Express* is a good example of an underground paper that did seek justice in the courts. Although *NOLA* won two cases and established an important legal precedent, government agents continued to make arrests and seize shipments, knowing the harassment was effective even if the charges were later dropped.

NOLA Express was an important political voice in New Orleans. The paper specialized in the ecological examination of the local terrain and in criticism of local nuclear power initiatives. Like many other counterculture papers of the period, *NOLA Express* linked artistic and political strategies, publishing avant-garde poetry and fiction, with writers like Charles Bukowski and William Burroughs. While *NOLA Express* was engaged in the publication of new literary and political ideas, the FBI was busy keeping track of *NOLA Express*. Documents released in 1979 under the Freedom of Information Act prove that the paper was under continuous surveillance by the FBI. FBI files contain testimony from confidential informers about printers, distributors, writers, and the political affiliations of staff members. John Sinclair, an important activist in the White Panther Party, was, among many other contributors to *NOLA Express*, a target for FBI surveillance. *NOLA Express* was forced to suspend publication in 1974 because it was evicted from its office and was putting money into a court case against a proposed nuclear power plant. Even after the demise of the paper, the FBI followed the staff. An FBI memorandum of January 21, 1976, noted that *NOLA Express* editors were back in New Orleans to find a printer for a new publication, *Evolution and Energy*.[44]

In 1969, *NOLA Express* and *Logos*, another New Orleans underground paper, won an injunction against the arrest of vendors, but within months a *NOLA Express* vendor was

NOLA, like other papers with adversary political content, was harassed for printing the same advertisements that ran in establishment media.

"Ad" satirizing *Playboy* taken to court.

arrested for "failure to move on." A United States District Court found the arresting officer in contempt of the injunction.

The history of *NOLA Express* was punctuated by government interference. An important case brought against the paper in 1969 attempted to prove that *NOLA Express* was mailing obscene material. The Federal District Court dismissed the charges on First Amendment grounds. The Court said that the item provoking the charges — a photograph of a nude man masturbating above a caption reading, "What sort of man reads *Playboy?*" — was designed to ridicule rather than incite prurient interest. The Court further ruled that a publication is obscene only if the entire work is sexually explicit material:

> . . . It is newsprint, evidently intended for social commentary . . . It represents a relatively new medium of political and social discussion in this country, sometimes called the underground press. In their newspaper, defendants urge a radical departure from the generally accepted way of life, and they use new and radical means of expressing their point of view. Judge Clark's conclusion with regard to the banning of *Lady Chatterley* from the mails is directly applicable here:
>> "In short, all these passages to which the (United States Attorney) takes exception — in bulk only a portion of the book — are subordinate, but highly useful, elements to the development of the author's central purpose. And that is not prurient."
> For these reasons I hold that the material that defendants are charged with mailing was constitutionally protected . . .[45]

Although the case established an important legal precedent for the distribution rights of underground newspapers, the trial produced unfortunate side-effects: the paper was forced to censor itself in order not to jeopardize ongoing litigation.

POLICE OBSCENITY

Hoping to eliminate the alternative media, the city of Milwaukee passed a tough, new obscenity law. It was immediately used to arrest John Kois, the editor of *Kaleidoscope*. He was fined $2,000 and given two years probation.[46] Probation was an indirect means of censorship because the writer or editor became liable for any printed material that the court might construe as a probation violation.

A Milwaukee COINTELPRO memo of 2/14/69 outlines how the FBI suggested exposing two teachers at the University of Wisconsin, Milwaukee, for writing articles in a paper which the agency called "extremely pornographic in nature." The FBI proposed arousing public outrage for "permitting instructors at that school to engage in this type of activity."[47] The editor, publisher, and cartoonist at the University of Hartford *Liberated Press* were all arrested for violating a Connecticut obscenity statute after they published a caricature of Nixon as a large, erect index finger.[48]

Police often used charges of pornography or obscenity to dismantle an entire publishing operation. In Dallas, the vice squad raided the office of *Dallas Notes* twice in the fall of 1968. The publisher was arrested, and two editors were intimidated into quitting. Armed with search warrants for "pornography," the police confiscated typewriters, cameras, darkroom and graphic equipment, business records, a desk, a drafting table, and all the copy for the next issue.[49] The police never had to demonstrate how a drafting table could be considered "pornographic."

SABOTAGE OF NEWS SERVICES

The FBI and its allies also concentrated on underground news services. COINTELPRO documents reveal that the FBI constantly spied on the Underground Press Syndicate and the Liberation News Service, which sent information bulletins and news stories with a radical perspective to subscribing journals. The FBI directed the IRS to investigate the tax records of Liberation News Service. In a typical FBI "dirty trick," its New York office in 1968 tried to interfere in a leadership dispute in the Liberation News Service by sending anonymous letters to New Left and other progressive political organizations impugning the motives of the LNS factions. The FBI document on this plan contains an apology to the Director because the forged letters were "written in the jargon of the New Left, necessitating the use of a certain amount of profanity."[50]

The Alternative Press Syndicate (formerly the Underground Press Syndicate), an underground information and advertising clearing-house, was another victim of government suppression. It helped establish new papers, organized the defense of member papers against government action, and maintained an extensive library of underground literature. In 1969, UPS served a combined readership of twenty million. Cindy Ornstein and the late Thomas Forcade, Project Coordinator for UPS, were under constant surveillance. They were arrested while covering the 1972 Miami convention.[51] In 1969, the Phoenix office of UPS, run by Forcade and *Orpheus* magazine, was infiltrated by a narcotics agent, who worked on the staff for six months. After he quit, local police raided the office with a warrant for illegal drugs. A thorough search, however, failed to turn up any drugs. In the course of the search, the police stole UPS subscription lists, destroyed files, and damaged the UPS library. Among the destroyed files were the legal records from underground papers which were being given legal aid by the UPS. When Forcade and UPS moved to New York, they continued to be harassed by FBI agents.[52] On one occasion, Cindy Ornstein was arrested for violating a firearms act, and UPS material was confiscated in the process.

In 1970 after repeated disruptions by government agencies, Thomas Forcade published a passionate open letter to the President's Commission on Obscenity and Pornography, to which he added a list of forty-five underground papers that had been victims of censorship.

UNDERGROUND PRESS SYNDICATE

Box 26, Village P. O.   New York, N. Y. 10014 (212)691-6073

STATEMENT   May 13, 1970

By: Thomas King Forçade, Projects Coordinator, Underground Press Syndicate

To: Commission on Obscenity and Pornography, Washington, D.C.

The Constitution of the United States of America says, "Congress shall make no law...abridging freedom of speech or of the press." This unconstitutional, illegitimate, unlawful, prehistoric, obscene, absurd Keystone Kommittee has been set up to "recommend advisable, appropriate, effective, and constitutional (??) means to deal effectively with such traffic in obscenity and pornography." To this we say, fuck off, and fuck censorship!

This Keystone Kommittee, engaged in a blatant McCarthyesque witch hunt, holding inquisitional "hearings" around the country, is the vanguard of the Brain Police, Mind Monitors, Thought Thugs, Honky Heaven Whores grasping to make thought criminals out of millions of innocent citizens. You ARE 1984, with all that that implies. This phony Kommittee begins with the pornography and obscenity existing in the eyes of the bullshit beholders and ends with total state control of the mind of every man, woman, child, hunchback and midget. What pretentious arrogance to presume, what colossal nerve to attempt to impose your standards on the public, while you jack off in the censorship room. Fuck off, and fuck censorship!

Either we have freedom of the press......or we don't have freedom of the press.

The Underground Press Syndicate has repeatedly encountered your brand of political repression in the thin but transparent guise of obscenity, despite the obvious fact that the primary content of Underground Press Syndicate papers is political and social writing. This becomes even more obvious when underground papers are compared to the millions of tons of specifically salacious and prurient four-color crotch shot magazines which are readily available in the same cities where underground papers are repeatedly busted for "pornography". We know where that's at, and we know where you're coming from. Beside, arousing prurient interest in America IS a socially redeeming value. So fuck off, and fuck censorship.

A study of daily newspapers found that 70 per cent of the readership did not believe the papers they read. They thought they were lying. In the past 20 years, over 400 establishment dailies have died, while in the past four years, U.P.S. has gone from nothing to over 6 million readers. A journalism professor in California made a study of his class of 45 students, and found that 42 read the local underground paper, only 1 read the establishment propaganda organ. The head of the American Association of Advertising Agencies warns the straight papers to "get in touch" or they will lose their advertising revenue to the underground press. But the can't "get in touch", because they are lackeys of a power structure whose only touch is a Midas touch, which tries to turn war into money, natural resources into money, even whole segments of our population into money.

The Underground Press Syndicate is fighting this, and winning, and you are terrified because we are robbing the power structure of its replacements. You are a dying breed, because young people love the underground press, live it, and know that it speaks the truth. But you walking antiques are constantly trying to stomp out our freedom of the press-uptight Smokey the Bears of the totalitarian forest, rushing around with shotguns for shovels, trying to quench the fires of freedom. But the fire is out of control, and we will not be brought down. America's Children for Breakfast program - youth genocide - is not working. To it we say, fuck off, and fuck censorship.

You politically self-ordained demi-gods have decided to jam two copies of the Reader's Digest into every shithole in America, with your dried-up, perverted, ugly, bland, middle-aged, hypocritic, jack-off, psychopathic, totalitarian, un sexed, dictatorial, Bank of America, warped, hyena, rancid, muck of your own decaying existence you make me puke green monkey shit.

In opposition to this, our program is liberation - total freedom - and we are totally committed to carrying out this program. A dictatorial structure cannot withstand the absolute power of a media that can turn out a half million people at Woodstock or a million people to sit on Nixon's back porch until the war ends. And we will no more passively accept the suppression of that voice than we will of our bodies.

We are the solution to America's problems. We are revolution, these papers are our lives, and nobody shall take our lives away with your goddamned laws. We are tomorrow, not you. We are the working model of tomorrow's paleocybernetic culture, soul, life, manifesting love, force, anarchy, euphoria, positive, sensual, communal, abandoned, united, brotherhood, universal, organismic, orgasmic, harmonious, flowing new consciousness media on paper, coming from our lives in the streets. So fuck off, and fuck censorship!

We are in charge of our own lives, and we bear allegiance only to our own Free Nation. We hold your ancient myths of sterile blue laws in utter, scum bag contempt for jamming up the river of human progress, trying to hold back, push back, compartmentalize, ram down our throat your death trip of thought control, the last perversion of Babylon. And the straight media is equally responsible, for they bear the guilt of the crime of silence, the crime of inaction as they watch and cheer while their media brothers in the underground press go down the drain of lost freedom of the press. They mouth empty words and they are total hypocrites.

There can be no free country without a free press, and if there be no free country, then there will be no country. There is no difference and no separation between what is happening to the underground press and what is happening to the Black Panthers or any other group which opposes America's last crazed epilepsy. The Underground Press Syndicate has been harrassed unrelentingly since it was founded in 1966, yet it has grown from just 5 papers and less than 50,000 circulation to over 200 papers and circulation over 6 million. For every paper destroyed by a bust, 10 more have taken its place, and if the message of that is not clear, then you must surely have to learn it by experience.

Congressman Joe Pool, late HUAC chairman, said, "The plan of this Underground Press Syndicate is to take advantage of that part of the First Amendment which protects newspapers and gives them freedom of press." Bob Dylan says, "Without freedom of speech I might be in the swamp." I say, "Write On!"

I do not agree with a word that you say, and I will defend to my death my right to say it...

Boycotted publisher Bill Schanen takes his stand in Port Washington

The Obstinacy of Bill Schanen

Life recognized the courageous stand for First Amendment rights taken by Wisconsin businessman Bill Schanen. "*Kaleidoscope* has merit," he said. "I don't agree with a lot of it but what are we supposed to do, get rid of everything we don't agree with? There is an issue here that is much larger than Bill Schanen."

INTIMIDATION OF PRINTERS

Many underground newspapers had difficulty finding a willing printer. Local political pressure, the threat of boycotts by advertisers and customers, and the printer's own political orientation often resulted in a refusal to do business with underground newspapers. In some cases, printers' unions dictated that members could not handle the work of underground publications. There is evidence that the FBI was behind some of these obstructions. *Orpheus* was refused by thirty printers; the *East Village Other* and *Rat* were turned down by countless printers on the East Coast. A New Jersey printer who originally had an agreement with *Rat* later reneged after the state's Attorney General threatened prosecution for obscenity.[53] Some papers were forced to cross state lines to find a printer. A printer agreed to accept the *Seattle Helix* only if the work was done secretly. After a visit from the FBI, the regular printer of the *Los Angeles Free Press* refused to continue. *The Rag* was turned down by several print shops in Austin. One printer who did accept its business delivered an issue with blank pages and black boxes masking sections he thought were obscene. COINTELPRO documents later revealed that at least one of *The Rag*'s printers was persuaded to stop printing the paper after a visit by San Antonio FBI agents.[54] A memorandum of October 13, 1970, from the Detroit FBI office proposed "the disruption of the physical plant of the Radical Education Project," a publisher of New Left documents.[55]

In Port Washington, Wisconsin, William F. Schanen, Jr., of the *Ozaukee Press* took on the publication of dozens of midwestern underground newspapers, refusing to comply with FBI and local advertiser demands that he keep away from allegedly subversive projects. He lost nearly $200,000 per year in printing business and advertising in his three establishment papers because he brought out *Kaleidoscope* and other alternative papers. A local industrialist and the American Legion retaliated by leading a boycott of Schanen's papers and of his advertisers. By 1970, Schanen was printing papers from as far off as Omaha, indicating the difficulty these papers had in securing printers.[56]

Not all printers were as resistant as Schanen to government pressure. In 1980, the Emergency Coalition to Defend Student Rights at Cleveland State University received declassified FBI documents exposing the complicity of a printer with the federal agency in spying on underground papers. The FBI memorandum reads, in part:

> . . . furnished the following information: . . . advised that his company will not publish any material containing obscene words or highly critical of the United States. [*Name deleted*] advised however, that apparently due to his contacts with schools, he gets numerous requests to publish "underground newspapers." He stated that the most recent such newspaper was [name deleted]. He advised that this newspaper is severely critical of the United States and the last edition thereof contains numerous obscene words. He stated that this paper is put out by an individual by the name of [name deleted]

> [Name deleted] then read both the second and the first edition and found them both to be very critical of the United States and the second edition had a considerable amount of obscenity. He printed the second edition, but deleted the obscenity therein. He then told [name deleted] to go somewhere else to do the rest of his printing. He advised that on September 29, 1970, an individual by the name of [name deleted] of Columbus, Ohio, brought in a tabloid, the name of which he could not remember, all pasted up and ready for printing, which he wanted printed. This paper was etremely [*sic*] smutty and extremely critical of the United States. Therefore, he refused to print it . . .

> [Name deleted] advised that in the future, when such papers are brought in, he will make a proof copy thereof and furnish this to the FBI, along with the name and address of the individual furnishing it to him. He will not print such material, however. He advised that he will notify the FBI when such material is brought to him.

The FBI also approached advertisers and investigated progressives who provided financial backing for underground papers. The agency wrote spurious letters when it was convenient. In 1969, the Detroit FBI office sent a letter to local advertisers signed "Disgusted Taxpaper and Patron" objecting to the content of one paper. In December, 1970, the Mobile FBI office sent an anonymous letter to a university administrator and threatened to expose two instructors who were providing money for a student counterculture newspaper. This action was intended to make the journal "fold and cease publication," to "eliminate what voice the New Left has in the area."[57] The two instructors were put on probation.

HOUSING INTERFERENCE

COINTELPRO memoranda also reveal that the FBI pressured landlords to evict journalist tenants. The Los Angeles FBI field office reported its measures to get two New Left papers evicted in 1968.[58] The same year, in New York, the FBI persuaded the landlord of *Rat* to double the office rent, forcing the paper to move. In Austin, Texas, the city condemned *whatever* building *The Rag* rented for its office. Fearing condemnation, landlords refused to rent to the paper.[59]

DRUG ABUSE OR DRUG EXCUSE

Richard Nixon made the issue of drug abuse a cornerstone of his "law and order" program in 1969. Local politicians and police agencies saw it was politically expedient to use drug laws to silence underground newspapers. It was easy to focus on drug abuse because drugs were considered a political issue by many in the counterculture. There is no question that drugs were widespread in countercultural communities and among the staff members of underground publications. Movements for the legalization or decriminalization of marijuana grew out of early advocacy of this cause in

IS WAR WITH RED LSD

No, says an intelligence analyst who argues that has replaced War

Private Flying: Therapy Aloft for Disab. d

The New Defense Secretary Thinks Like the President

ARGENTINES FORCING HAIRCUTS ON HIPPIES

Special to The New York Times

BUENOS AIRES, Jan. 27 — The Argentine federal police disclosed this weekend that, since the current campaign against hippies began earlier

Narcotic Chief Charges With Dope Law Laxity

■ **Drug Control:** The President urged stiffer penalties for merchants of "slavery to the young"—traffickers in LSD and other "dangerous drugs" and a 30 per cent increase in the number of Federal narcotics agents. Outlook: excellent

Wall Street took on the role of the anti-hero (just like in the new movies) last week. It played awfully rough with the young and old heroines who are investors, as stock prices plunged lower than a starlet's decollete. But, when things got really bad, it came to the rescue and kept its cool during the Korean crisis.

The faces on the cutting room floor were those of timid souls who panicked Thursday morning, when news of the call-up of reserves reached brokerage house boardrooms. The tape-watching in-and-out traders who sit studying stock prices (their feet planted firmly on the floor to hide the holes in their shoes) reacted as expected to their breed.

But just when that kind of news indicated that the nation is finally heading back toward vigorous business recovery (after last year's slump) the usually over-optimistic Commerce Department played the villain. They took a look at their charts and pronounced that their "leading indicators of future economic activity" looked weaker in December than in November. They're telling us that, just maybe, things aren't as rosy as the lads in Endsville-on-the-Potomac had thought.

OUR HEAVIEST RUBBERIZED PADDING!

THE NEW YORK TIMES, FRIDAY, JANUARY 26,

PESSIMISTIC ON VIETNAM: Senator Edward M. Kennedy in Boston telephoning his Washington office yesterday. In his first public address since his trip to Vietnam, he cited growing resentment among Vietnamese refugees.

ASK TO MEDITATE

East Village Other

BLACK MARKET RESEARCH

Last April, EVO published a questionnaire aptly titled "BLACK MARKET RESEARCH," which sought to obtain a statistical sampling of the ways and means of drug usage among our readers. We asked for truthful answers, with no unnecessary bullshit. The response was beautiful. Some were neatly typed, crisp facts. Others were ebulliently decorated with flowery designs, obviously executed in a state of total groove.

·Our thanks to Theo Solomon, whose computer was invaluable.

The figures quoted have been computed from a total of slightly more than 1,200 answered questionnaires.

1. Do you or have you ever smoked or taken the following:

Marijuana	98%
Hashish	85%
Cocaine	31%
Peyote	41%
LSD	77%
Psylocybin	12%
Heroin	21%
Laughing gas	23%
DMT	50%
DET	14%
STP	3%
Methedrine	70%
Diet Pills	55%
Bananas	19%
Pepper and food stuffs	10%
Darvon	4%
Barbiturates, tranquilizers	18%
Morning Glory seeds	10%
Opium and Morphine	11%
Demerol	3%
Cough Medicine	4%
Glue	3%
Codine	5%

2. If you answered yes to any of the above questions, which to your knowledge do you consider your worse trip or evil?

LSD	10%
STP	2%
Methedrine & Amphetamine	22%
Diet pills	5%
Marijuana	3%
Food stuffs & Morning Glory	5%
Peyote	4%
Barbiturates	2%
Cocaine	2%
Heroin	19%
Cough Medicine	1%
glue	2%

3. Which do you consider your best trip:

Marijuana	44%
Hashish	27%
LSD	28%
DMT	7%
Peyote	5%
Methedrine & Amphetemines	1%
Morning Glory	0
Cough Medicine	1%
Laughing gas	1%
Psylocibin	1%
Heroin	1%

4. If you smoke marijuana, at what age did you start?:

0 - 12	2%
12 - 14	4%
15 - 16	21%
17 - 18	25%
19 - 21	29%
22 - 25	13%
26 plus	6%

B. Do you smoke everyday:

Yes	27%
No	51%
No Response	21%

C. Do you smoke only at night:

Yes	14%
No	65%
No Response	21%

D. Do you ever smoke too much:

Yes	25%
No	66%
No Response	9%

E. Did you ever have a hangover:

Yes	18%
No	73%
No Response	9%

F. Do you have a steady connection:

Yes	55%
No	36%
No Response	9%

G. Is your connection a fe:

Yes	13%
No	62%
No Response	25%

H. How much do you pay per ounce:

$5	11%
$6 - $10$11 - $15	16%
$16 - $20	15%
$21 - $25	33%
Over $25	6%
No Response	3%
	15%

5. How much do you spend per month on grass:

$5	9%
$6 - $10	10%
$11 - $15	7%
$16 - $20	15%
$21 - $25	4%
Over $25	13%
Over $50	6%
Over $100	1%
Free through selling	5%
Free by gift	6%
Free - growing	2%

6. How do you prefer to take your marijuana:

Joint	46%
Pipe	33%
Water Pipe	30%
Food	7%

7. Have you ever sold drugs — including marijuana:

Yes	64%
No	31%
Sell under special circumstances	5%

8. Do you consider your drug use religious:

Yes	22%
No	62%
Sometimes	16%

9. Do you practice it alone or in a group:

Alone	9%
Group	22%
Both	59%

10. Do you consider it a ritual·

Yes	15%
No	71%
Sometimes	14%

11. Do you drink alcohol or beer:

Yes	44%
No	34%
No Response	22%

12. What do you do when you turn on - type of activity:

Sedentary Yes	44%
No	8%
Both	25%
No Response	23%
Sensory Yes	51%
No	49%
Emotional Reaction	
Positive	60%
No Reaction	40%

13. Activities while turned on:

Social	24%
Sexual	33%
Creative	25%
Intellectual	38%
Routine	42%

15. Are you very paranoid because you use drugs:

Yes	14%
No	54%
Both	32%

16. Do all your friends turn on:

Yes	28%
No	72%

17. Ever busted for dope:

Yes	13%
No	87%

18. Age:

0 - 12	1%
13 - 14	0
15 - 16	3%
17 - 18	11%
19 - 21	28%
22 - 25	35%
26 - 30	12%
30 plus	10%

19. Sex

Male	69%
Female	31%

20. Education

Grade School	2%
High School	4%
High School graduates	22%
Part college	29%
B.A. B.S. degrees	29%
Some graduate work	7%
Graduate degree	6%

21. What do you do for money:

Work	45%
Supported by parents	12%
Partime work	29%
Sell dope	14%
Unemployed	7%
Student	7%

East Village Other 1968.

the underground press. All this made it easier for police to obtain search warrants to raid alternative press offices. If no drugs were found in a raid, as was often the case, other material was confiscated or photographed. CIA, FBI, and military intelligence agents who had infiltrated underground papers, or groups who worked with them, informed narcotics squads when drugs were being used. Tom Forcade of the Underground Press Syndicate observed that the rate of arrest of underground journalists for drugs was one hundred times the general rate of narcotics arrests.[60]

Newspapers had good reason to fear infiltration by police agents. Staff morale was undermined by the anxiety and distrust bred by the chance that narcotics agents might be among them. Often people were arrested, then offered suspended sentences in exchange for information.

A state-of-siege atmosphere prevailed in many alternative newspaper offices. In 1968, the St. Louis *Daily Flash* printed a series of articles critical of police chief Walter Zinn. An undercover police officer was assigned to infiltrate the *Flash*. A short time later the police agent arrested an editor, Pete Rothchild, for suspected possession of marijuana.[61] The Ann Arbor *Argus* ceased publication in 1970 when the entire staff was arrested on charges of drug possession, following an editor's arrest on an obscenity charge. The two-year-old paper had a circulation of 15,000. The editors of *Rat* and the Minneapolis *Free Press* were arrested, the *Free Press* editor sentenced to five years in prison for the possession of marijuana. After being arrested twice on pornography charges, then convicted for inciting riot, Stoney Burns, art director and founder of *Iconoclast*, was sentenced in Dallas, in 1972, to ten years and one day in prison for the possession of less than one-tenth of an ounce of marijuana. The extra day in the sentence prevented eligibility for parole.[62] Within a year, public protest freed editor Burns.

Perhaps the best known case in which drug laws were used to silence radical writing was that of John Sinclair and the Artists' Workshop in Detroit.[63] Sinclair had helped found the Artists' Workshop in 1964. During this period of growing racial separatism, it served as a meeting ground for the

The Dramatics

The Battle of Pontiac

Who Killed King?

Goodbye Hound

Leonard Woodcock

In the Vortex:
Albert King
Terry Callier
Rufus
Joni Mitchell

«KULCHUR»

CoatPuller
Bill Hutton
Calendar

and much more

Serving Metropolitan Detroit and Greater Michigan

SUN

Volume 4, No. 1 · January 22, 1976

WHO RAN THE S.L.A.?

The Symbionese Libera-tion Army, which kidnap-ped Patricia Hearst in Feb-ruary 1974, was a creation of several government agen-cies, including the CIA and the California Department of Corrections. Its leader, Donald DeFreeze, was an experienced police informer and *agent provocateur* who was allowed to escape from prison, then got out of hand. Patty Hearst had visited him in prison and discussed kid-napping her younger sisters.

Prison authorities forced inmates in several California institutions to recruit for the SLA on the inside, then contributed names of other inmates to its "death list." At least thirteen prisoners have been killed by SLA "soldiers."

A former FBI agent claims to have been asked by the agency to take DeFreeze's place in the SLA and to have made contact with Hearst underground. The SLA received guns and money from a Los Angeles *agent provocateur* who of-fered them incentives to commit further acts of terrorism.

Was the SLA created and developed in order to asso-ciate left-wing groups with terror and violence? Read the first substantial investi-gative report on the SLA, following page 8, and decide for yourself.

10th Precinct Prosecution: "Stupid & Incompetent" – p.3

Busing in Detroit:
DeMascio Goes Through the Motions

One of the most extraordinarily limited school busing plans yet for-mulated in the U.S. is finally scheduled to go into effect in Detroit on Monday, January 26. After Judge Roth's original metropolitan busing plan was turned down by the U.S. Supreme Court, federal District Judge Robert DeMascio began a process of gradually watering down proposals by the NAACP and the Detroit school board, leaving us with a plan that will bus less than 10 per cent of the city's school popula-tion. Many all-black city schools, the worst in the city, remain un-touched by the so-called "desegregation" program.

Most close observers expect implementation to be comparatively smooth—and why shouldn't it be, with the suburbs, the heart of the segregation problem, left out? There are still anti-busing groups with-in the city, but politicians are less willing to stick their necks out these days for them, and fortunately, there is no longer an Irene McCabe to offer dynamic leadership.

Although the Detroit area has had a stormy past in busing, it would be a mistake to frame the present issue in terms of the potential for violence. Busing has been so used and abused by the straight media,

Turn to page 2

Behind Angola:
Why the West Wants Africa Back

By Alexander Cockburn and James Ridgeway

With hair flying and fists pummeling the rostrum, the portly U.S. ambassador to the UN, Mr. Daniel Patrick Moynihan, bellows out his denunciations of the "Soviet colonization of Africa."

In his fear-sodden imagination, he sees vast Soviet armadas domin-ating the waters around southern Africa; he sees the rich argosies of the Soviet merchant marine ploughing their way back to the Russian motherland, laden with African loot: gold, diamonds, molybdenum, cobalt, ivory, and all the other treasures of the dark continent.

He sees a Communist swathe bisecting Africa, red communes wher once the tribal chieftains and the Peace Corps held sway.

He sees white South Africa put to the sword, a link up of black communism with insurgent Latin America, the swift isolation of the United States, and finally the triumph of the Third World, dancing to the Soviet tune.

This nightmare he shares with his master, Henry Kissinger.

There's some truth to this madness. There is a recolonization of Africa going on. And indeed the Russians and the Chinese do have a

Turn to page 6

reconciliation of blacks and whites. An energetic cultural center, the Workshop produced the newspapers *Guerrilla* and *Sun*, books of poetry, a literary magazine, *Work*, news and jazz reviews. Allen Ginsberg and Sinclair were among its many contributors. On June 24, 1967, the Artists' Workshop Press was raided by local, state and federal narcotics officers and U.S. Customs Agents. Fifty-six members of the Workshop, including Sinclair, were arrested on testimony by two undercover narcotics agents who had infiltrated the Workshop. The charges against most Workshop members were dropped. Sinclair, however, was found guilty of possessing two joints' worth of marijuana. Although his arrest was protested by many writers and literary groups, including PEN American Center, he was sentenced to ten years imprisonment, the longest term ever given in Michigan for a similar offense. He was denied bail during the appeals process. At the time of his imprisonment, Sinclair was editor of the *Sun*, a writer for the Ann Arbor *Argus* and *Fifth Estate*, Minister of Information of The White Panther Party, and was a widely published poet. While serving his sentence, Sinclair, with two others, was accused of conspiring to bomb the Central Intelligence Agency office in Ann Arbor. The government case, resting on testimony of a double agent, subsequently failed in court.

LOVE &
ENERGY =
WORK⁴

edited by
John Sinclair

Artists' Workshop
Press/Detroit

FBI: TO END AMICABLE BLACK AND WHITE RELATIONS

DE 100-35108   Confidential

       The specific suggestion is that a letter could
be written from the BUF at Washington, D. C. to the White
Panther Party (WPP), 1510 Hill Street, Ann Arbor, and also
to the "Michigan Daily", University of Michigan student newspaper at Ann Arbor, pleading the BUF cause. The letter which
could possibly be initiated by an informant in the BUF in
Washington, D. C., or which could be a fraudulent letter could
ask the WPP, a white militant group that strongly supports
the Black Panther Party (BPP), to help the BUF collect the
just and modest sum of $25,000.00 from the NMC by making a
direct overture to ███████████, an NMC leader in Ann
Arbor. The letter could state that the BUF realizes that a
substantial part of this sum could be easily raised by the
NMC in Michigan because of the many professional and academicians
supporting the anti-war demonstration scheduled for Washington,
D. C. The letter could also state that a copy is being directed
to the University of Michigan student newspaper to further
publicize the very just nature of the BUF request.

       Detroit feels that the "Michigan Daily" would be
delighted to publish this type of a letter. It is felt that
such a letter would be of a disruptive nature if presented
to the Detroit Coalition Committee by ███████ and could
develop into a situation where ████████████████████████
████████████

       Such a letter would also be a disruptive factor to
the amicable relations between the WPP and Black Nationalist
supporters and groups in Ann Arbor, inasmuch as WPP would be
forced to make a choice between BUF cause and the position
of the white liberals in Ann Arbor who have been critical
of the war and have to this point supported the WPP. The
issue in the letter would be that the BUF knows that the
white liberals, who are identified with the NMC, have unlimited sums of money available through their contacts and
the sole issue is whether or not they want to give the
$25,000.00 to the BUF.

       Comments of WFO are requested. If the Bureau
approves of this suggestion, a draft of such a letter will
be prepared by Detroit.

Confidential

- 2 -

THE CREATION OF CONSPIRACY

The use of conspiracy and terrorist charges was part of an effective strategy to muzzle free speech. As in the Chicago Conspiracy Trial following the Democratic Convention of 1968, such charges were used to neutralize the influence of New Left and counter-culture leaders by embroiling them in lengthy and expensive trials. Nebulous conspiracy laws allowed prosecutors to harass dissidents by bringing vague charges before a grand jury, with the accusation almost always resulting in acquittal. As centers for counterculture and reform activity, underground publications were vulnerable to prosecution for conspiracy. New Left political activists— often editors and writers—were accused of directing alleged terrorist activity from news headquarters.

The Juche Cooperative of Cambridge, Massachusetts, was virtually destroyed by police agents acting illegally in a spurious search for terrorists. The Cooperative was the center for many self-supporting community activities, including a food cooperative, a clothing exchange, a bookstore, and a forum for poetry readings.It also produced *Juche*, an underground newspaper which reflected the grass-roots radicalism of the Co-op. On November 17, 1970, the center was raided by police; the next day the Boston *Record American* carried the headline: " 'Revolutionary' Den Raided." The co-op members were charged with illegal possession of firearms and conspiracy to violate the firearms act. In fact, the weapons found in the center were legally registered and had been purchased for protection after repeated threats from right-wing vigilante groups. In the course of the raid, typewriters, books, subscription lists, and personal belongings were seized.[64]

INCITEMENT TO RIOT

Government paranoia in the wake of the bombing of Haiphong in 1972 resulted in a flurry of "incitement to riot" charges against underground journalists. Four writers from the Columbus *Free Press* were charged with *causing* the riot they covered. They were jailed for a week with total bail set at $100,000. It took a year before they were acquitted of the felony charge.[65]

Stoney Burns, editor of *Dallas Notes*, was charged with inciting a riot after his arrest in 1970 during a confrontation between young people and the police in a Dallas park. Shouting, "There's the one we want, right there," Dallas policemen grabbed Burns, clubbed him, and took him to jail. The riot charge was later changed to "interfering with an officer during a civil disturbance." Burns was convicted and sentenced to three years. This was not the first time Dallas police had clashed with the editor. In two earlier raids, police had confiscated *Dallas Notes'* property. Incoming mail addressed to staff members was often marked "Opened by mistake by U.S. Marshal's Office." *Dallas Notes* was banned on the Southern Methodist University campus, and students at North Texas State University in Denton were arrested for distributing an election issue. Before raiding *Dallas Notes*, police had Southwestern Bell Telephone disconnect the telephones. The paper's offices were twice attacked by organized vigilantes, who destroyed typewriters and printing equipment. At least three times shots were fired at Stoney Burns' car. Dallas police repeatedly stopped and searched automobiles owned by the workers. A Fort Worth man told Burns he had been hired to assault Burns physically. In view of the fact that Burns was later sentenced to ten years imprisonment for a minor drug offense, the charge of terrorist activity — inciting riot — proved to be just one of several tactics used to stop him and *Dallas Notes*. In filing suit on Burns' behalf, the Dallas Civil Liberties Union charged that ". . . the conduct on the part of the Dallas police is part of a conspiracy having as its object prohibiting the expression of ideas that are alien to the defendants, and having as its ultimate goal the abolition of *Dallas Notes*."[66]

The persistent persecution of Burns stemmed in part from Burns' 1967 investigative report in Dallas Notes about Texas Congressman Joe Pool's arrest for drunken driving, after his car hit a carload of soldiers at a red light. Pool was released and the arrest records destroyed after police realized who Pool was. The story did not appear in the big Dallas daily newspapers. In fact, the Dallas *Morning News* and *Times Herald* responded to the *Dallas Notes* report by reporting Pool's statement that the underground newspapers would "slander and libel everyone who opposes these traitors [the underground press] in their attempts to destroy American government."[67] COINTELPRO documents petitioned by the Underground Press Syndicate reveal that Pool, a member of the House UnAmerican Activities Committee, called for an investigation of underground newspapers. These official records go on to state that Pool "has already made a major plank of his re-election campaign in Dallas the harassment of 'Notes from Underground' (*Dallas Notes*)."[68]

Articles exposing wrongdoing by political officials triggered attacks on underground newspapers in Philadelphia, including the use of terrorist charges against them. In 1968, after publishing several articles critical of the Philadelphia Police Department and its commissioner, Frank Rizzo, the *Distant Drummer* was charged by Rizzo with solicitation to commit murder. The District Attorney refused to prosecute, claiming that printing these articles did not constitute a crime.[69] When the Philadelphia *Free Press* published damaging information about Rizzo and the police department, Rizzo vowed to destroy the *Free Press* just as he had the local Students for a Democratic Society (SDS) and the Student Nonviolent Coordinating Committee (SNCC). Between February and August, 1970, the Philadelphia Police Department assaulted one *Free Press* staff member, held several others in detention without charge, searched four staff members' homes without warrants, broke into their locked cars, confiscated political literature on narcotics warrants, and opened mail. At least six police cars at a time tailed *Free Press* staff members. In addition, police agents visited employers, advertisers, and the paper's printer. As a result, one staff member lost his outside job, the paper's printer refused to continue, and many advertisers withdrew their business.[70] On July 28, 1970, the Philadelphia *Evening Bulletin* ran a major story on the *Free Press*, calling staff members "violent" and "hardcore revolutionaries." Material for the article came from Philadel-

istant rummer

NEWS FROM THE JUNGLE

NUMBER 10 15C

20¢ OUTSIDE PHILA/PUBLISHED AT 315 SOUTH 13TH STREET, PHILA
MEMBER UNDERGROUND PRESS SYNDICATE/LIBERATION NEWS SERVICE

phia police and FBI files and from Selective Service records. The story gave confidential financial, family, and employment information about people who worked for the *Free Press* and attempted to link them with Weather Underground bomb factories and the Cuban government.[71] This portrayal of the *Free Press* as an advocate of violence and murder threatened to drive the paper out of business. More people were fired from their regular jobs, and because no new advertisers replaced those lost, the paper's free distribution was jeopardized.

In a hearing before the Senate Subcommittee on Internal Security in 1970—called to discuss "attacks" on local police by activists—Sen. Thomas Dodd announced his sponsorship of a bill that would "prohibit publication of periodicals that advocate violence against lawmen and overthrow of the Government." The *Black Panther Party Paper* and *NOLA Express* were cited as examples of violent publications. Sen. James Eastland introduced a similar bill, making it a federal offense to incite others to cross state lines to assault a police officer. Police from several states testified at the hearing, and endorsed the effort to prevent the circulation of the Black Panther paper.[72]

NOLA EXPRESS

NEW ORLEANS, LOUISIANA, NUMBER 123, JANUARY 19 - FEBRUARY 1, 1973, SECOND CLASS POSTAGE PAID, 35¢ OR BARTER

THE CASE FOR A NUCLEAR MORATORIUM

A NEWSPAPER OF DETROIT
March 19 - April 1, 1970
Vol. 4, No. 23 (101)

20¢
IN DETROIT
25¢ Elsewhere

COPS OF AMERICA · · ATTENTION

WOULD RICHARD NIXON DIE FOR YOU ?

"Both police and armed forces follow orders. Orders. Orders flow from the top down. Up there, behind closed doors, in antechambers, in conference rooms, gavels bang on tables, the tinkling of silver decanters can be heard as icewater is poured by well-fed, conservatively dressed men in horn-rimmed glasses, fashionably dressed American widows with rejuvinated faces and tinted hair, the air permeated with the square humor of Bob Hope jokes. Here all the talking is done, all the thinking, all the deciding."

--Eldridge Cleaver
Soul on Ice

MORE DIRTY TRICKS

Legal, financial, and psychological intimidation were common tactics, but it was very difficult to prove that the police had actually been acting illegally. Since the demise of many papers was due to trial expenses rather than actual convictions, the police could continue to harass writers and still keep their hands clean. However, when prosecutions proved unsuccessful, some agencies resorted to violent action. In communities where underground papers were a real political force, agents sometimes committed brutal assaults on papers and staffs. The larger and better-established underground newspapers seem to have received the brunt of the physical harassment possibly because they held up better under legal attacks than the smaller, more vulnerable journals.

Kudzu, produced in Jackson, Mississippi, served as a major organizational center for the New Left and counterculture in that area. The tenacity of the paper and its allies can be gauged by the fact that by 1968 the newspaper had survived a conviction on obscenity charges, the arrest of salespeople, the confiscation of cameras, and even eviction from its offices. On October 8, 1968, eighteen staff members and supporters of *Kudzu* were attacked and beaten by Jackson deputy sheriffs. At the same time, the FBI was planting information with one of its "friendly" media contacts at the Jackson *Daily News* for an article condemning the New Left. COINTELPRO documents record the fact that this article was made into a pamphlet to be distributed to local schools by the American Legion.[73] In 1970, *Kudzu* was put under direct surveillance by the FBI. For more than two months, FBI agents made daily searches without warrants, claiming to be looking for SDS leader Mark Rudd and for Brandeis students accused of robbing a bank. On October 24 and 25, *Kudzu* sponsored a Southern regional conference of the Underground Press Syndicate. The night before the conference the FBI and Jackson detectives searched the *Kudzu* offices twice. During the search, an FBI agent threatened to kill *Kudzu* staffers. On the morning of October 26, FBI agents again searched the offices. That evening local police entered the

KUDZU 25¢

JUNE 1970
VOL. 2 NO. 7

FREEDOM AND JUSTICE SUSPENDED IN MISSISSIPPI

IN THIS ISSUE:

BOYCOTT
HUEY NEWTON FREE?
LA. FEST RAIDED
JOHN LEE HOOKER

building, held its eight occupants at gunpoint, produced a
bag of marijuana, then arrested them. After conflicting police
testimony, the eight were released. This intimidation followed
the appearance of a series of articles in *Kudzu* concerning the
police shooting of students at Jackson State College the
previous May. Moreover, in October, *Kudzu* had exposed an
FBI provocateur, who had bombed a building at the University of Alabama. A *Kudzu* staff member commented,
"The FBI used to be fairly sophisticated, but lately they
have broken one of our doors, pointed guns in our faces, told
us that 'punks like you don't have any rights,' and threatened to shoot us on the street if they see us with our hands in
our pockets."[74]

In many cases, violent acts were committed against underground newspapers while the people responsible for those
acts were never identified. The fact that these acts of violence
occurred in the midst of law enforcement actions against the
same underground newspapers, however, cannot be overlooked.
Police harassment of underground newspapers certainly encouraged groups intent on carrying out their own vendettas.
These groups often assumed that their actions would either
be condoned by the local police or, at the very least, that they
would not be prosecuted. In fact, there were very few arrests
made in connection with attacks on underground newspapers.
When offices were firebombed, officials rarely intervened to
protect the victims or to apprehend the perpetrators.

When the Los Angeles *Free Press* was bombed three
times, police made no effort to investigate the crime While
Dallas Notes was under heavy police surveillance, it was
raided twice by right wing groups. In Houston, *Space City
News* was bombed in 1969 during a systematic campaign of
violence against white political activists and black liberation
groups in the area. The Ku Klux Klan was believed to be responsible for the bombing. The Houston Police Department
conducted only lax, inconclusive investigations of the bombings and shootings. Ironically, the same police agencies were
accusing left progressive groups of engaging in "terrorist"
activities and subverting American "law and order." In fact,
much of the right wing terror was generated by FBI provoca-
teurs working in groups like the Ku Klux Klan.

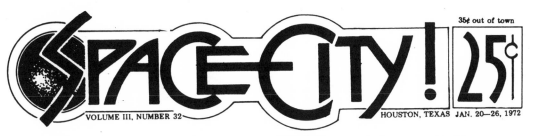

VOLUME III, NUMBER 32

35¢ out of town

25¢

HOUSTON, TEXAS JAN. 20—26, 1972

SECOND CITY

POLITICAL AND LITERARY REVIEW

15¢

CHICAGO, ILLINOIS   PUBLISHED BY THE GUILD COOPERATIVE FELLOWSHIP   NOVEMBER 1972 VOL. 3, NO. 10

In most cases it was impossible to determine who planted the bombs used against underground newspapers. The co-ordination of bombings with authorized police campaigns suggests they were carried out by police agents or groups who knew officers would turn the other way. When the offices of *Orpheus* in Phoenix were bombed unsuccessfully, the police finished off the job, destroying UPS files. After Atlanta's *Great Speckled Bird* won its obscenity trial in 1972, its offices were fire-bombed.[75] The office of the Washington, D.C. *Free Press* was ransacked just before the presidential inauguration in 1969. It wasn't until 1973 that the *New York Times* reported that Army intelligence agents and the FBI had participated in the raid.[76]

SECOND CITY AND THE "LEGION OF JUSTICE"

Facts have recently surfaced, revealing that some attacks on underground papers were made by right-wing vigilantes in collusion with law enforcement agencies. A gang of thugs calling itself the "Legion of Justice" terrorized New Left and counterculture groups in Chicago while police looked the other way. From the day it began in 1968, *Second City*, the newspaper published by the Guild Bookstore, was under surveillance by the Chicago Police Department. At a party for the first issue, police burst in and announced that *Second City* would be watched by an intelligence unit called the Red Squad. The following year police detained *Second City* vendors, who were selling papers in compliance with local statutes.

Then, in November and December 1969, Legion of Justice vigilantes attacked Socialist Workers Party headquarters in Chicago and Dekalb, destroying property, beating people, and stealing files. *Second City* was the only Chicago paper to publish a full account of the incidents. Therefore, it was not surprising that on February 3, 1970, four men from the Legion of Justice sprayed the Guild Bookstore with tear gas. They overturned bookshelves, threatened the bookstore attendant, and threw a dummy hand grenade as they fled. A few days later, a *Second City* street vendor was assaulted by three men, whom he later identified for the police. The police did not apprehend these men, members of the Legion of Justice. Instead they suggested the vendor come back the next day to swear out a complaint. That day, two of the thugs returned to the Guild bookstore, threatening an editor of *Second City* and another worker. When asked to get out, they burned a hole in the worker's jacket.

On March 11, five members of the Legion tried to disrupt a "war crimes tribunal" being held at a Chicago theatre. The Red Squad kept an eye on the proceedings until a few minutes before the arrival of a Legion gang, at which time the police unit retired to squad cars outside. When the thugs began breaking up the meeting, the officers refused to intervene with the excuse: "We aren't city cops—we're Red Squad."[77] Participants in the tribunal, two of them from *Second City*, finally evicted the Legion members. Later, the police charged the tribunal participants with assault.

Police and vigilante coordination seemed routine. On March 13, eight Legion men converged on the Guild bookstore, threatening the lone attendant several times. When he held up a legally registered gun to protect himself, a dozen police officers appeared with guns drawn. The book clerk was arrested for aggravated assault and possession of an unregistered gun. The assault charge was later dropped. (The Legion failed to appear in court.) And the Guild employee was acquitted because the gun was legal. Whenever the Guild bookstore and *Second City* pressed charges for assaults by the Legion, the latter filed countercharges against its victims. On the two occasions when Legion members were convicted for their attacks on *Second City*, they were given minimal "good conduct" sentences and released. One of these terrorists was finally arraigned on major felony charges for the attack on the Socialist Workers Party.

The Legion of Justice had ties not only to the Chicago police but to other government officials. State Attorney General Edward Hanrahan, later indicted for conspiring to murder Black Panther Fred Hampton, resisted months of pressure from groups calling for an investigation of the Legion of Justice. Robert Boyle, Assistant State Attorney,

SECOND CITY

25¢

Chicago, Illinois   Vol. 2, No. 6

HANRAHAN PROTECTS TERRORIST GANG

HUE, 1968: Vietnamese civilian killed by American artillery shell. Photo by an ex-Navy photographer who wishes to remain anonymous.

did meet with a citizens' committee investigating neo-Nazi vigilantes, including the Legion of Justice. He discovered afterwards that their discussion had been electronically monitored. Boyle informed the citizens' group and soon afterward resigned from office. Peculiar links between the Legion of Justice and city administrators kept showing up. The editor of *Second City* found that confidential information she gave the state counsel in a case against Legion members ended up in the hands of the Legion's founder and defense attorney, S. Thomas Sutton.

Information released since 1970 reveals that the Chicago Police's Red Squad also worked in close cooperation with the Army's 113th Military Intelligence Group. The Red Squad's accomplices in the Legion of Justice received money, tear gas, mace, and electronic surveillance equipment from the 113th.[78] Several times, material stolen in Legion burglaries found its way to the Military Intelligence Group.[79] This included defense documents stolen from the attorneys in the Chicago Conspiracy trial. Army agents acted as observers in that burglary. Chicago police, in testimony before the Senate Committee on Intelligence, disclosed that a fire had destroyed Red Squad files, housed in police headquarters, during a probe of that intelligence unit.[80] The CIA (through the Law Enforcement Intelligence Unit) also worked with the Chicago Red Squad and the Legion of Justice. The CIA and the Chicago Red Squad exchanged surveillance information through LEIU. In addition, the CIA trained spies for the LEIU. A CIA memorandum of February 8, 1973, listed some of the briefings and training seminars held for LEIU agents. Between October 6 and October 8, 1967, Chicago police participated in "demonstrations of explosive devices, an exhibit of foreign weaponry, air operations, and paramilitary displays . . ." The CIA trained them in "surreptitious and non-surreptitious entry" and in electronic surveillance. In several instances, the CIA provided the police departments with the equipment required for these operations.[81]

"... IN THE INTEREST OF JUSTICE"

The Milwaukee and Madison *Kaleidoscope*, which together had a circulation of 30,000, were the objects of violent attacks that seem related to simultaneous legal prosecution. An FBI COINTELPRO memorandum of February 14, 1969, proves that the Milwaukee *Kaleidoscope* was under FBI surveillance.[82] While editor John Kois was on probation in the late 60s for his obscenity conviction, his car was bombed and shot at. The newspaper office also was bombed and its windows shattered by gunfire. *Kaleidoscope*, more than other alternative journals, seems to have been persecuted more for exercising normal press freedoms than for the content of the material printed. Photographer Gary Ballsieper was arrested four times for disorderly conduct while taking pictures for the journal. He and Kois were arrested in Chicago covering the antidraft trial of the Chicago 15. They were jailed with the defendants and temporarily charged with conspiring in their case.[83]

Kaleidoscope was instrumental in one of the most important tests of press freedom. It was probably attacked because it made a policy of exposing undercover agents working in the area. The January 20, 1970, issue of the paper published the names, addresses, and photographs of three military intelligence officers conducting surveillance around Madison. In late August, the paper printed a statement by the New Year's Gang claiming responsibility for the August 24 bombing of the Army Mathematics Research Center on the University of Wisconsin campus. A grand jury subpoenaed *Kaleidoscope* editor Mark Knops, asking him to disclose the source of the New Year's Gang statement. Knops refused on the grounds that the press could not be required to reveal its sources. Judge Erwin Zastrow sentenced Knops to six months in jail for contempt of court, stating, "What has to give is the First Amendment privilege—in the interest of justice." Knops served one month and was released when he agreed to answer six questions unrelated to the source of his story. One hour after his release he was subpoenaed again and this time ordered to reveal all his news sources. On refusing, he was sent back to jail.[84] In December, after having served four

CONSTITUTION ATTACKED

See Page 3

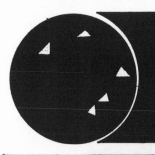

kaleidoscope©

milwaukee, wisconsin

member: underground press syndicate (u.p.s.)
liberation news service (l.n.s.)

months, Knops was released on bond by a federal judge pending appeal. The reaction of the established dailies to this case was mixed. A September 4, 1970, editorial in the Chicago *News* took the position that the contempt charge was correct, citing Attorney General John Mitchell's "temporary guidelines" for certain circumstances. The Chicago *Sun Times*, on the other hand, defended Knops' right to withhold his sources. The Milwaukee *Journal* initially sided with the contempt charge, but after the second subpoena and Knops' return to jail, the paper backed Knops, saying a demand for all sources was a threat to all reporters and an illegal use of grand jury powers. On November 7, the Milwaukee chapter of the professional journalist society, Sigma Delta Chi, issued a resolution condemning Knops' imprisonment.

The *Kaleidoscope* case shows how underground papers were forced to struggle for the simplest press rights. It was virtually impossible for critics of the government to get press passes to major events and press conferences. For several years Tom Forcade was the only underground reporter with press clearance for the House and Senate.

In some cases, the State tried to silence alternative journalism by arguing ownership of information. In 1970, the editor and a writer for the Los Angeles *Free Press* were convicted of receiving stolen property—that is, information—from the California Attorney General's office. This property consisted, in fact, of a xeroxed list of state narcotics agents that a government worker gave the *Free Press*. When the paper published the names and address of some of these agents, it was taken to court by the Attorney General and fined $10,000. Defense attorneys argued that information does not qualify as property, citing as precedent a case in which Drew Pearson had been acquitted for reporting "stolen" information about Senator Thomas Dodd. The court had ruled that the press cannot be limited to publishing only information about the government which the government itself issues.

This same issue has resurfaced in 1981, with government attempts to silence the *Covert Action Information Bulletin*, Philip Agee, and others who publish names of U.S. intelligence agents. The Agent Identities Protection Act, proposed in both houses of Congress, makes it a federal offense to publish classified or unclassified information which may be used to disclose intelligence operations or the identities of intelligence agents. Intelligence agencies would become the sole source of information about themselves.

In May, 1972, Ron Ridenour, of the Los Angeles *Free Press*, was arrested while covering an anti-war demonstration in front of CREEP (Committee to Re-elect the President) headquarters. Two police officers pushed Ron Kovic, a paraplegic Vietnam veteran, from his wheelchair and began to beat him. When Ridenour shot pictures of the incident, from fifteen feet away, the police confiscated his camera and arrested him for unlawful assembly and interfering with a police officer. He was convicted and sentenced to a year in jail. When his camera was returned, the film had been exposed.[85]

In 1971, Tom Miller, a freelance writer for the Underground Press Syndicate, *Rolling Stone*, and other journals, was subpoenaed by a federal grand jury to testify in its Tucson hearings on the Weather Underground. The Justice Department refused to allow Miller the exemption customarily allowed reporters because he was a freelance writer and an activist. Before this issue could be resolved, the original grand jury disbanded.[86]

TARGET: PANTHERS

The U.S. government saw the Black Panther Party as the center of black liberation struggles in the country, and the FBI kept it under constant surveillance. It was a prime target of COINTELPRO operations; documents show that 233 of 295 authorized COINTELPRO actions against black groups were directed against the Panthers. Among the crimes committed by the government in dealing with the Party were spying, wiretaps, forged defamatory letters, disruptions of meetings, provocation of dissension, gang wars and, finally, murder.

The *Black Panther Party Paper* was harassed by the government because it was the Party's chief means of circulating information and bringing in income. The *Paper*'s salespeople were arrested repeatedly by Buffalo police for violating a state criminal-anarchy statute. The FBI forged anonymous letters and sent them to school officials protesting the presence of the paper in the library and classrooms.[87] In 1969, a federal grand jury ordered Sherry Bursey and Brenda Joyce Presley, Panther newspaper staff members, to disclose confidential information about the management of the newspaper. The two refused, and they were later upheld by an appeals court.[88] In 1970, a House subcommittee investigating the Black Panthers asked Frank B. Jones, a former managing editor of the paper, to furnish details about circulation, distribution and finances.[89]

Not only was the Black Panther Party destroyed by government agents, but underground papers were not allowed access to report the trial of Party members in New Haven in 1971. A group of writers formed an Ad Hoc Committee for a Public Trial to protest their being denied access to the trial by a "conspiracy"[90] of the Nixon administration, the Federal Bureau of Investigation and the State of Connecticut.

FBI: WHOSE "ANGRY BLACK BROTHER"?

F B I

Date: 8/25/69

Transmit the following in _____
(Type in plaintext or code)

Via   AIRTEL   _____
(Priority)

TO: DIRECTOR, FBI (100-449698)

FROM: SAC, DETROIT (100-35108)(P)

SUBJECT: COINTELPRO - NEW LEFT

ReBuairtel to Detroit, 8/20/69, captioned as above.

Detroit proposes utilizing the following counter-intelligence technique as a disruptive measure within the BPP/SDS. An anonymous letter would be sent to local and national leaders of these organizations, with particular emphasis on the prominent SDS activists, and BPP leaders in the Detroit Division.

This letter will be signed "An Angry Brother" and will read as follows:

"Dear Brothers and Sisters

"Since when do us blacks have to accept the dictates of the lillywhite SDS? To do so would only further hinder Party progress, in gaining black control over black people. We have had more than we can tolerate of white pig facist control over our destiny. We are sick and tired of being severely brutalized and denied our civil rights and treated like animals by white facist police departments. To hell with SDS and their white 'intellectual' approach of whites controlling everything. There is only one answer to our problems and that is to follow and enforce by any means necessary the Black Panther Party theory for community control over all police departments regardless of color. SDS is a paper organization providing lip service rather

2 - Bureau (RM)   1 - San Francisco (RM)
1 - Detroit   1 - Chicago (RM)
WWW:LMO
(5)

Approved: _____   Sent _____ M   Per _____
          Special Agent in Charge

DE 100-35108

> than the forceful and violent tactics rightfully employed by the Panthers. Let's completely break away from any affiliation with SDS and continue to pursue our aim of 'all power to the people'.

> "An Angry Black Brother"

San Francisco and Chicago are requested to offer any suggestions re above proposed anonymous letter.

In furtherance of developing effective disruptive techniques aimed at causing friction between SDS/BPP, Detroit will consider utilizing its contact with ████████████, Detroit News, a local newspaper with a circulation of 800,000 - 900,000 copies. For the information of the Bureau and other interested offices, this contact in the past has been utilized with considerable success.

Information furnished to Mr. ████████ relating to this matter will be of a public source nature and would not in any way expose the Bureau as being involved. Bureau authority would be specifically requested before any contact of ████████ was made.

Detroit further porposes that informants be instructed to make statements aimed at causing disruption in SDS/BPP, in an effort to further widen the gap between these two organizations. These informants, if authorized to make the above type statements, would be instructed to deal with issues that in no way would expose them as informants and would be designed so as not to subject them to any retaliatory measures by the BPP/SDS.

FBI: ON THEIR BACKS

OPTIONAL FORM NO. 10
MAY 1962 EDITION
GSA FPMR (41 CFR) 101-11.8

UNITED STATES GOVERNMENT

Memorandum

TO : DIRECTOR, FBI   DATE: 5/18/71

FROM : SAC, ALEXANDRIA (100-624) -P-

SUBJECT: OFF OUR BACKS NEWSPAPER
WOMEN'S LIBERATION MOVEMENT
WASHINGTON, D. C.
SM - MISCELLANEOUS
(OO:WFO)

   Enclosed for the Bureau and WFO is one copy each
of Off Our Backs newspaper, Volume I, Number 22, for 5/27/71.

   For information of the Bureau, the captioned news-
paper has been printed by the Journal Newspapers, Inc., 331
North Fairfax Street, Alexandria, Va., since 1/71, for Off
Our Backs, Inc., Washington, D. C., Women's Liberation
Collective.

   On 5/17/71, ████████ advised the most recent
edition of Off Our Backs was printed on 5/12/71, and furnished copies of which are included with this communication
as enclosures.

   The Bureau is being furnished a copy of this paper
due to an article which appears on Page 17, entitled "3 Most
Unwanted--F.B.I. Story." The article, authored by SUE STRAUSS
of the Federal Employees For Peace, is in regard to the three
former FBI clerical employees, LINDA JANCA, CHRISTINE HOOMES,
and JANICE BUSH, who recently resigned in protest of a matter
of Bureau policy.

(2) - Bureau (Enc. 1)(By Courier)
2 - WFO (Enc. 1)(By Courier)
2 - Alexandria (1-100-624)
  (1-170-199A)
WAL:sw
(6)

Buy U.S. Savings Bonds Regularly on the Payroll Savings Plan

WFO 52-¿1203

███████████ went to the offices of "Off Our Backs" and
an individual who would only identify herself as a "staff
member" of "Off Our Backs", advised that that paper has a
strict policy regarding non-cooperation with the FBI, and she
furnished no information to the agents and terminated the
interview.

ARMED AND DANGEROUS - EXTREMIST

Long after COINTELPRO authority had ended, the
FBI carried on as usual. The Socialist Workers Party suit in
1976 revealed continuing wiretaps and burglaries.[91] Recently
released FBI documents show FBI surveillance of the *Independent
Eye* of Cincinnati during July, 1975, just before the
newspaper went under. Commenting on this recent disclosure,
the agent now in charge of the Cincinnati FBI office stated
that the Bureau could not investigate political groups "unless
there is evidence of criminal conspiracy."[92] The FBI has so often
found criminal conspiracy where it does not exist, this statement
is not reassuring.

Documents released in 1978 concerning the paper *Off
Our Backs* (Washington, D.C.) show that the government
spied on women's publishing concerns. A memorandum from
the Washington, D.C., FBI office to the Director suggests
incorporating an investigation of *Off Our Backs* into an ongoing investigation of the women's liberation movement.[93]
Another memorandum proposes surveillance of the newspaper
to determine printing and publishing facilities, circulation,
funding, leading members, New Left connections, propensity
for violence, and "whether individuals reside in a communal-
type existence."[94] Other FBI communications discuss the
printer and financial problems of the paper. A July 2, 1973,
memorandum reports that a staff member of *Off Our Backs*
would not cooperate with an agent's investigation. This is
followed by the designation "ARMED AND DANGEROUS—
EXTREMIST."[95]

The Persecution Of The STREET JOURNAL
As Conducted By
C. Arnholt Smith And James S. Copley

A classic example of government efforts to muzzle an underground newspaper is the case of the San Diego *Free Press and Street Journal*, founded in 1968 by The People's Commune. The commune also operated a retail store, Peoples' Dry Goods, which sold works by local artists and craftspeople, published handbooks and pamphlets, supplied office space to the Movement for a Democratic Military, and provided five-cent dinners for San Diego citizens in need. All this was going on in a community dominated by a large U.S. Navy presence, a strong John Birch Society, two daily papers owned by conservative James S. Copley, and a business community headed by financier D. Arnholdt Smith, a major fundraiser for Richard Nixon and Ronald Reagan. The *Street*

Journal's troubles began after one of the first issues exposed the corrupt, Mafia-related deals of a prominent businessman, who was later imprisoned for his crimes.[96] In October, 1969, the newspaper picked up a story reported in the *Wall Street Journal* (but unreported in the Copley papers) concerning the large profits made by D. Arnholdt Smith at the expense of other stockholders in transactions with public companies he directed. Smith was reported to have reacted to the *Street Journal*'s story by saying, "I wish there was some way to bomb them clear to the other side of the Coronados."[97] Soon afterward, the bombing began.

A suit filed by the *Street Journal* and the Peoples' Commune in 1970 against the San Diego Police Department, the City of San Diego, and officers of both lists attacks on the newspaper between November 1, 1969, and February 24, 1970.[98] In a single month, twenty street vendors were arrested for "obstructing the sidewalk." Vendors of other publications, in the same locations, were not arrested. In December, 1969, a municipal court ruled the obstruction ordinance to be unconstitutional, but police continued to make arrests on the same charge. On November 18, 1969, bullets were shot through the windows of the paper's editorial offices. The incident was reported to the police, but they took no action on it. On November 23, five San Diego squad cars surrounded the offices of the paper and police searched the office twice without a warrant, arresting seven members of the Peoples' Commune on various charges. The charges were later dropped.

On November 29, 1960, the glass door to the *Street Journal*'s editorial office was smashed and 2,500 copies of the current edition stolen. This occurred during the period San Diego police were keeping watch on the commune. When staff formally reported the incident, the police once again did not investigate. On December 1, the *Street Journal*'s landlord received telephone calls demanding the paper's eviction. Throughout this period, commune members and other tenants of the building received bomb threats. The police were informed and did not investigate. The newspaper was forced to find new offices and reached an agreement with one Billy Joe Reeves. On December 14, a San Diego police officer asked Reeves to cancel the lease as "a personal favor." Reeves refused but he agreed two weeks later after being arrested on a murder charge. He was detained for an hour, and his offices were searched. Commune members later learned that the murder suspect being sought was five feet, eight inches tall, weighing 175 pounds, while Reeves was five feet, three inches tall, and weighed 114 pounds.

On December 11, 1969, two police officers, without a search warrant or consent, entered and searched the *Street Journal* and arrested a friend of the commune members on suspicion of burglary. The victim was handcuffed and taken away, then released without being booked. On December 25, hoodlums invaded the editorial offices, stole business and subscription records, and destroyed expensive typesetting equipment. The police were informed and did not investigate. On January 3, 1970, a car belonging to a *Street Journal* writer was fire-bombed. When informed, the police threatened to impound the car at the paper's expense if it were not removed from the street. On January 9, police impounded another automobile, owned by a commune member and legally parked, for remaining in the same location for seventy-two hours. The day before, a driver of that same car had received a ticket for a traffic violation in another part of San Diego. The next day a *Street Journal* staffer got a ticket for an invalid driver's license, even though he had, in fact, shown the officer a valid license. On January 15, 1970, six police officers and four United States Navy Shore Patrolmen entered the newspaper's premises without a search warrant or consent. They interrogated people from the commune, opened envelopes, files, and address books, copied information, confiscated personal property, and threatened physical violence if the victims attempted to communicate with a lawyer. On January 6 and 15, street sellers were arrested for violating nonexistent laws. On January 17, a commune member, just discharged from the Navy, was arrested for wearing a military jacket. He was held for fourteen hours and interrogated before charges were dropped. On January 18 and 25, three vendors were arrested for littering and held on $1,500 bail. On February 4, San Diego police and Shore Patrolmen again illegally searched newspaper offices and arrested staff members on phony charges, later dropped. On February 8, they attacked the Peoples' Commune again, threatening residents and searching the premises. They smashed in the door and seized and dragged one person outside, though he was never accused of wrongdoing. Throughout the period of harassment, police routinely confiscated coin-operated vending machines owned by the *Street Journal* and held them at the police department.

The *Street Journal*'s suit ends with the charge: "During the latter part of 1969 and 1970 to date, plaintiffs are informed and believe and therefore allege that officers of the said San Diego Police Department have kept plaintiffs under almost constant surveillance, in violation of plaintiff's rights of privacy, and that, included in such surveillance have been the use of wire taps, hidden microphones, and infrared photography, and that said surveillance has been conducted without any warrants or orders of the courts, or any reasonable, legal or probable cause whatsoever."

Harassment did not end when the lawsuit was filed. The searches continued, automobile tires were slashed, and the windows of stores selling the paper were smashed. A federal grand jury was convened in an attempt to indict the *Street Journal* on charges of "criminal syndicalism," a law used to crush organization and publication by the Industrial Workers of the World in San Diego in 1919. The law had been declared unconstitutional in 1950.[99] Finally, the pressure of constant surveillance and intimidation forced the *Street Journal* to close down. It took nearly a year for the suit filed by the paper to be heard, by which time most of the plaintiffs had moved, and the suit was dropped.

Having annihilated the *Street Journal*, the San Diego right-wing coalition then turned to the San Diego *Door*. When it followed the path of the *Street Journal*, it too was attacked. Cars were firebombed, and office windows shot out. On one occasion, arsonists set the newspaper's office on fire, destroying typesetting equipment and almost killing a staff member.[100] During this period, the two established daily newspapers in San Diego made almost no mention of the attacks on underground papers.

On June 21, 1971, a movie theatre showing X-rated movies was bombed while two San Diego police officers were sitting in the audience. An investigation found William Francis Yakopek to be the bomber and a member of the Secret Army Organization (SAO), the militant wing of the Minutemen, a far-right paramilitary group. The investigation also exposed Howard Berry Godfrey as a leader of the SAO and an FBI informant. Subsequently, Godfrey was called on to testify before the Senate Select Committee on Intelligence concerning the relationships among the SAO, the FBI, and the San Diego Police Department (SDPD). Godfrey told how the FBI and SDPD organized, trained, and equipped the Minutemen and SAO. Godfrey said he instructed the SAO in guerrilla warfare, locksmithing, propaganda techniques, and security and intelligence procedures. He gave information to the FBI in exchange for funds for SAO activities. Godfrey admitted that his group was responsible for firing on the *Street Journal* offices, smashing the windows of a store selling the *Street Journal* and *Door*, and stealing 2,500 copies of the *Journal*. In collaboration with a San Diego police officer who had infiltrated the *Street Journal* staff, the SAO destroyed the typesetting equipment and stole the newspaper's records.[101]

Information released over the years provides a disturbing picture of a coordinated effort to silence the *Street Journal* and other underground publications.[102] In San Diego, local business leaders, the city police force, the district attorney, the U.S. Navy, the FBI and a paramilitary group all conspired against the constitutional rights of the free press. Long before this conspiracy was brought to light, however, its object had been accomplished.

San Diego
FREE PRESS

San Diego 20¢   Sept. 3 - Sept. 17   ◄►-   Vol. 1 No. 22 Issue 22   Elsewhere 25¢

SERVICEMEN: This news-
paper is your personal
property. It cannot be
legally taken from you!

COPLEY PRESS

INDICTED FOR SMUT !

ON PAGE 6

DUCKS TORPEDO NAVY

ON PAGE 4

ARTAUD -

WANTED FOR THE

MURDER OF WESTERN CULTURE

ON PAGE 7

siné

THE MILITARY CAMPAIGN

"SELECTIVE SERVICE CITES LIST OF REASONS FOR REJECTION FROM ARMED FORCES" — News Item

HOW TO GET IN OUT OF THE DRAFT

BY WALTER

FROM THE CHICAGO SEED [UPS]

Uptight with The Draft? Find out the other side. Draft Information Center

THE MILITARY CAMPAIGN

The war in Vietnam aroused opposition not only among civilian writers, but among members of the armed forces, who began their own underground papers. During the 1960s and 1970s, anti-militarism and anti-imperialism were forcefully expressed by the thousands of draftees pressed into fighting in Southeast Asia. Unable to tolerate dissent, military authorities worked relentlessly to drive military underground publications out of existence.

Given the great power granted the military command over its ranks, it is astonishing how many underground papers there were. The insulated nature of military life allowed military commanders to use their full authority to control the voice of dissent among servicemen. Intimidation by rank, the right to transfer, to demote, imprison and simply make life miserable were common tactics in the campaign against the freedom to write. Military authorities censored authorized military media so that GIs received only the information sanctioned from above. The issues at stake in the censorship of *unauthorized* military media were not only the right to receive and disseminate information, but the right of military personnel, as United States citizens, to express political opinions when not on duty. Censorship of the alternative newspapers clearly violated First Amendment rights of people in the armed services who wrote for and read those publications.

To control these underground publications, the command used disciplinary, judicial, and surreptitious tactics. Intimidation by rank and threats of prosecution by military courts often provoked self-censorship among writers in the military. Those who exercised their right to publish and write were harassed and verbally abused by their superiors. Sometimes they were transferred without advance notice, demoted to menial assignments, and followed by military police and intelligence. The close ties that military intelligence had with the FBI and local police were helpful in monitoring the activities of armed forces members. These organizations cooperated in the surveillance of anti-war groups and publications staffed by soldiers and civilians. An FBI memorandum from J. Edgar Hoover to the FBI office in Chicago requested an immediate investigation of people working for *Vietnam GI*, published in Chicago. The May 3, 1968, request states: "A review of the attached edition of the *Vietnam GI* indicates that it is of a seditious nature."[103] The FBI, the Washington, D.C., Police Department, and even the sanitation department in that city, cooperated with Naval intelligence in spying on and hounding Roger Priest, publisher of *OM*.

FUN, TRAVEL AND ADVENTURE

The first unauthorized newspaper of the Vietnam war era was *The Bond: The Voice of the American Servicemen's Union*, issued in 1967. This was followed by the newspapers *Fun, Travel and Adventure* at Fort Knox, Kentucky, and the *Fatigue Press* at Fort Hood, Texas.[104] By 1970, the presses of sixty underground military newspapers were rolling. Generally written by GIs for GIs, they spoke out against the war in Vietnam. Many papers supported the American Servicemen's Union, which called for reforms in the military, including the election of officers by vote of the soldiers, racial equality, the right of free political association, and the right to disobey illegal orders.[105] Articles outlined the rights of military personnel, described the process of obtaining conscientious-objector status, and documented the harassment of dissident GIs. Poems, short stories, and drawings by military personnel were often printed in these papers.

The regular apparatus for maintaining order and discipline gave the Armed Forces extraordinary powers of control in the campaign to silence military underground newspapers. GIs produced independent journals during their free time. Because they were printed on privately-owned equipment, they were outside the jurisdiction of the military command. So efforts to control the underground press had to be channeled through disciplinary structures of the armed forces that were established to prosecute breaches of military regimen and were not intended to apply to off-duty activities. Military

THE
BOND

The Voice Of The American Servicemen's Union

VOL. 5, NO. 10 New York, N.Y. **OCTOBER 29, 1971**

by Sp/4 Greg Laxer (ret.)

Recent developments have made plainer than ever the kind of "freedom and democracy" our brother GIs are dying to "defend" in Indochina. "Vietnamization" continues to fail completely, Cambodian puppet Lon Nol has openly displayed his true face, the American people continue to demand an end to the war, and our rank-and-file brothers are taking the necessary steps to save themselves from needless slaughter. (See article on Fire Base Pace on this page.)

The people of South Vietnam have been victimized for over a decade by US troops under the command of profit- and glory-hunting generals and politicians. Many of the people joined the National Liberation Front (the so-called "Vietcong"), and most support it, so that most of the countryside was freed from the control of the US and its puppets in Saigon. Thus, the focus of US power became centered in the big cities, where the populace could more easily be kept under control. But this picture, too, is rapidly changing, and Nixon is on the verge of losing everything.

In the cities, Vietnamese workers have been staging strikes against exploitation at US-Saigon hands. Disabled war veterans demonstrate in demand of decent benefits. South Vietnamese President Thieu's "re-election" on October 3 brought the people to a new level of anger. Thieu's anticipated opponents, Vice President Ky and General "Big" Minh, dropped out of the "contest," knowing the results were to be rigged. In response to Thieu's unopposed "campaign," over 60 new mass organizations were formed in the cities to struggle for peace and freedom, and against dictatorship. Buddhist leaders called for a boycott of the "election," and students firebombed US vehicles. Thieu ordered his National Police to shoot to kill demonstrators. The US command restricted GIs to their bases during the "election" period to reduce anti-US incidents and to prevent sympathetic EM from showing support for the people.

On "election" day, the streets were crawling with troops in full combat gear. Soldiers were posted with loaded M-16s at every polling place. The New York Times quoted a cook in Saigon: "I'm afraid to go vote because there are so many soldiers in the streets. But I'm more afraid that they will arrest me if I do not vote." Many Vietnamese refusing to vote in past "elections" found themselves thrown into tiger-cage dungeons. To boycott the "election," then, took great courage, but many of the people did just that. Thieu, of course, claimed an 87% voter turnout and a "confidence vote" for himself of 94.3%! These claims were such gigantic lies that, despite increasing repression and censor-

(continued on page 8)

(reprinted from Workers World)

50,000 GI DEATHS
BUY THIEU'S
"RE-ELECTION"

GIs at Pace Say
"HELL NO!"
to Night Patrol

South Vietnamese demonstrators, protesting the "elections," battle an armored car and tear gas in Danang.

by PFC Pete Perkins (ret.)

Firebase Pace is one of several forward area artillery firebases built with taxpayers' money within firing range of the Cambodian city of Krek. Krek is a town on the Cambodian border famous for the many rubber plantations that surround it. American GIs are forced to fire endless rounds of howitzer fire across the Cambodian border in support of the illegal US war effort in Cambodia. The continuous shelling not only kills people and destroys their land, it also turns artillery crews into sleepless, walking zombies.

Not content with these tactics alone, the Brass have a special kind of operation called the night patrol. On a night patrol you go stumbling off into the darkness, amid the booby traps, with the intention of finding other soldiers to shoot at. Presumably, the Brass, flying over in helicopters, can tell if the other soldiers are "friendlies" or "enemies." With many ARVN troops in the area, it isn't surprising that 15 were killed recently by an "errant" US air strike. At any rate, it is your duty to stir up a firefight.

Firebase Pace falls uder the command of Maj. Gen. Jack J. Wagstaff, commander of US forces of the 3rd Military Region, and this pig has found himself with a fight on his hands. It should be pointed out that rubber plantations are plantations in the same respect that cotton plantations were (and still are) plantations, with rich, greedy plantation owners and super-oppressed workers. When armies of these oppressed people rise up and rebel against the oppression, pigs like Wagstaff are sent to meet this resistance with crushing force.

All was not going well for US forces and the puppet ARVNs and so, as the battle for Krek entered its second week, the men of Co. B, 1st Battalion 12th Cavalry, of the 1st Air Cav. Division were ordered onto a night patrol. This time the men refused. Specialist 4th Class Walter Wernli was quoted by national press as saying, "This patrol was completely senseless -- senseless suicide." SP4 Albert Grana wrote a letter of explanation and protest to Sen. Edward Kennedy saying in part, "We want to draw the attention of the American public to the situation...we are almost forgotten here, getting shot at from Cambodia and shooting into it, and a patrol would have possibly gone into Cambodia." The letter was signed by 66 men, read onto tape and taken out by Richard Boyle, a freelance writer.

After that the base was closed to newsmen and Company B was moved to another firebase. Wagstaff insisted that no refusal of orders had taken place (only a "small misunderstanding"), transferred the company to a less forward base and ordered an "investigation," called for by none other

(continued on page 8)

officials harassed individual soldiers by bringing disciplinary charges against them. In most cases these charges were entirely unrelated to the writing and publishing of dissident opinions, the offense for which the GIs were actually being punished.

The military police routinely confiscated shipments of military underground newspapers and harassed and arrested vendors. When dissident GIs were court-martialed for minor infractions of discipline, not only was their work with underground papers stopped, but their prosecution was intended to intimidate other GIs.

In August, 1969, for example, servicemen Henry Mills and John Lewis were stationed at Fort Dix, New Jersey, where they worked on the underground military newspaper *SPD News*. Both men were court-martialed on minor disciplinary charges. Mills was sentenced to six months imprisonment; John Lewis was fined for protesting Mills' arrest. Both men had to serve 76 days in the Fort Dix Stockade while awaiting trial.[106]

The military command also used its power to transfer staff members of underground papers. On January 25, 1970, an anti-war GI paper, *Anchorage Troop* was distributed near Fort Richardson and Elmendorf Air Force Base in Anchorage, Alaska. The following afternoon the military Office of Special Investigation (OSI) searched the editor's room without a warrant and seized copies of the newspaper, mimeograph material, and rough drafts of the next issue. The paper's editor, A1C George Edge, was then charged with violating Article 15 for an unmade bed, dirty floor, and improperly draped clothes. A court-martial was scheduled, but charges were dropped. Edge was at once reassigned to Kelly AFB in Texas and transferred there on less than twenty-four-hour notice. In this case, the efforts of the military command were thwarted, as *Anchorage Troop* stayed alive under another editor and Edge became the editor of *Your Military Left* in San Antonio, Texas.[107]

For the most part, the military used the same kinds of intimidation to silence dissent as it used to control other infractions of military discipline. In the case of underground publications, however, the Army went too far, harassing military personnel for actions the Defense Department had ruled to be consistent with military law. In September, 1969, the Department of the Army issued its "Guidance on Dissent":

> Dissent, in the literal sense of disagreement with policies of the government is a right of every citizen in our system of government; we do not ask that every citizen or every soldier agree with every policy of the government. Indeed, the First Amendment to the Constitution requires that he be permitted to believe what he will. Army regulations provide that personal literary efforts may not be pursued during duty hours or accomplished by the use of Army property. However, the publication of "underground newspapers" by soldiers off-post, and with their own money and equipment, is generally protected under the First Amendment's guarantees of freedom of the press. Unless such newspapers contain "language," the utterance of which is punishable under federal law (eg., USC Sec. 2387 or the Uniform Code of Military Justice), authors of an "underground newspaper" may not be disciplined for mere publication.[108]

A directive from the Assistant Secretary of Defense for Manpower followed, stating that military underground newspapers and demonstrations by personnel should be allowed, within limits, because "dissent in its proper sphere is healthy for the United States."[109]

The military command paid little attention. The large number of underground papers and dissident GIs active during the Vietnam war worried the Pentagon. According to the Church Committee report, military underground newspapers were a primary target of military intelligence, which usually tried to plant informants on paper staffs. In 1970, fourteen RITA (Resistance in the Army) groups were kept under watch. Those same years the Army monitored over fifty-three underground military newspapers.[110]

The Army's *domestic* intelligence program was exposed in 1971, and the public outcry forced the military to redefine the scope of its intelligence powers. The military argued that their abnormal powers came from the National Security Act of 1947, which gave to the branches of the service the responsibility of protecting the efficient functioning of those branches.[111] Military intelligence was intended to protect the service from threats to its operation. The command decided the "efficient functioning" of the military was disrupted by opposition to U.S. and Pentagon policies. In response to accusations that there was no way to prevent illegal surveillance of civilians, the Defense Investigative Review Council (DIRC) was established in 1971 to look into all proposals for military spying on the home front.

Because no guidelines were ever established as to what constituted a threat, DIRC approval was virtually automatic. For example, in October, 1971, DIRC approved a request from Air Force Secretary John McLucas to investigate an underground paper published in the vicinity of Travis Air Force Base in California, in order to determine the danger it posed to Air Force activity and property.

The Air Force Office of Special Investigations spent an entire year trying, unsuccessfully, to plant a spy on the staff. In the end, it had identified fifty Air Force personnel and fifteen civilians who worked on the paper. The office did not report finding any evidence of threatening, subversive activity.[112]

AT HOME AND ABROAD

Military intelligence activity was not restricted to U.S.-based military underground newspapers.In 1973, the Army attempted to infiltrate *Fight Back* printed in the university ambience of Heidelberg, West Germany. From 1972 through 1974, Army intelligence spied on the paper, *Forward*, published by civilians and service personnel in West Berlin. The Army placed informants on the staff and opened mail addressed to the newspaper. In Japan, the Naval Investigative Service

Vietnam GI

September, 1968 — STATESIDE EDITION — Free to Servicemen

FT HOOD STRIKE!

The action of 43 black EMs at FT Hood has set a precedent that may well be followed and improved upon by thousands of GIs in the future. On August 23, the 43 stopped going along with the Brass's game—they refused to be used to put down so-called "civil disturbances" in Chicago during the Democrat Convention.

Now the Brass are trying every trick in the UCMJ, as well as several new ones, to punish the demonstrators. *They're afraid millions of other GI's might get the idea they can buck the system and win. But the Army is finding that it's a lot harder to railroad 43 men who hang together than it is to screw them over one at a time, as they usually do.*

The demonstrators, many of them decorated Nam returnees, are members of the 1st and 2nd Armored Divisions at Hood. When they decided the time had come to make a stand, they issued a statement which said: "We won't go to Chicago or any place in the United States to put down a civil disturbance or riot by our black brothers."

The GIs began assembling on post at the intersection of 65th and Central on the evening of the 23rd. The group was orderly and quiet and expanded as the night wore on.

At 2 a.m. MAJ GEN John Boles, of the 1st AD, tried to talk the men out of staying. When that failed Boles, fearing the solidarity of the group, told the men they could continue demonstrating without repercussions. When asked to put his promise in writing Boles refused, but he raised his right hand and swore to it with his staff as witnesses.

At 5:45 a.m., however, a Colonel tried to break the General's promise. LT COL Edwin Kulo, 1st AD Provost Marshal, appeared and said, "I want you all to go back to your area." A couple of minutes later he added, "I'm asking you to leave now, otherwise the MPs will take you in." Again no direct order was given, only a request and a threat. The men remained solid and unmoving.

As MPs stood by, some of the men asked to see their lawyers and were refused. Shortly after, an MP Captain yelled 'get 'em" and the MPs attacked, screaming and swinging clubs. Many of the demonstrators were injured as they attempted to protect their heads from the blows. One, a wounded combat vet, demanded medical attention. He had difficulty breathing and his wounds were bothering him seriously. *Ten hours later, and only after he began urinating blood, he was finally treated.*

The Brass had not covered themselves, even under their own kangaroo code, by issuing any direct orders. But that screwup didn't seem to bother them. They singled out 8 of the 43 as leaders and set up general courts-martial on charges of disobeying a direct order! The 8 are now attempting to force the Brass to limit their prosecution to special courts-martial.

The remaining 34 (one other was not charged) are receiving special courts, many of which have now ended. They are being tried in groups of 6 and 8 at time. The brass are trying to ram through convictions by lying and other tactics. But the heaviest stockade sentence thus far has been 6 months; several have gotten 3 months or acquittals. Of the most recent group, as VGI goes to press, 4 out of 6 were acquitted.

There are several reasons for these "light" sentences (according to the usual standards.) There are the determination and aggressiveness of the GIs, and the fact that they have a civilian lawyer. The publicity about the case also makes it tough for the Brass to be as heavy-handed as they are when they're dealing quietly with isolated individuals. And there's no doubt that they fear the response of thousands of other GIs at Hood if they hand down extreme sentences.

But the Brass's case is too shabby even for convictions, much less extreme sentences. Some examples:

—Defense attorney Weldon Berry of Houston had the defendants sit in the spectator section at the beginning of the trials. Prosecution witness SGT Walton of the 501st MP Co stated, "I never forget a face," yet he picked out only one of the accused from among the spectators.

—High officers were called in to lie about the events. LT COL John J. Cassidy and LT COL John Saalberg testified that they heard COL Kulo give the 43 a direct order to disperse. But the Brass couldn't produce Kulo as a witness.

—Strangely enough, GEN Boles never appeared to testify about his promise.

—At one trial the defense called CAPT William R. Robbins, former senior aide to GEN Boles. He turned out to be the one officer involved who told it like it was.

Robbins testified that he heard GEN. Boles tell the men that they could stay where they were gathered without fear of punishment, but that he had "advised" or "suggested" that they disperse. He also said that Boles told the men that if they did not want to go to Chicago, they should not have to go. But Robbins' testimony didn't matter, of course. It didn't fit the official Brass version that the LT COLs had testified to.

The Army is shook. FT. Hood is one of several recent events which shows that the little brass dictators are facing a new kind of enlisted man—and they haven't figured out how to deal with him. The general courts of the 8 men who were singled out are yet to come. But the events thus far are themselves a victory for EMs everywhere.

If the trend continues—and thousands of GIs can *make* it continue—the Brass will be unable to force GIs to fight in countries and cities, in wars that no one voted for and no one benefits from, except for the hawk corporations and their politicians.

The information for this article has been gathered by the staff of Fatigue Press, an underground sheet put out by GIs at Hood and from the staff of the "Oleo Strut," a coffeehouse run by GIs and sympathetic civilians in Killeen.

Murder At Benning

We know it's the job of the Army to kill men. But its own men?

On May 25, SGT Lon E. Baker died of "complications following heat exhaustion" after a five mile forced march at Fort Benning. The complications involved two officers on the march.

When Baker became unable to march any further, two officers dragged him along the road and beat him. When the medic told the officers that Baker might die, the reply was, "if he dies throw him in a ditch."

The two officers, LT Robert E. Lanham and CAPT Lance C. Warner were accused of maltreatment, assault, and dereliction of duty in failing to provide proper medical treatment. On Aug. 9, both officers were acquitted by a general court martial board after five days of hearings.

Baker had served five and a half years with the army, had been through the desert training program in California and had served a year in Nam winning a Bronze Star. He was a black man.

The march was part of an eight-week Ranger training course. The Ranger training program according to the Co COL Irwin Edwards "involves 1,075 hours of instruction. A student works in excess of 130 hours a week."

From the testimony revealed at the court martial, Baker had refused to take salt tablets before the march because they had made him sick in Nam. After marching four miles, Baker finally sat down in the road and said, he "wouldn't go any further and nobody can make me go any further." Lanham and another Ranger student got Baker up and pushed him along. When he fell a second time, Lanham dragged him about 65 feet. Then Warner and Lanham and a student grabbed Baker by his gear or "anything they could get ahold of in an attempt to get him to his feet." Baker tore away from his gear and started running. He fell into a ditch trying to pick up a stick. The medic got no reaction when he snapped his fingers in front of Baker's eyes. Dr. *Henry Busey testified that "a layman should have been able to recognize that Baker was sick."*

But the two officers, convinced that Baker was only trying to avoid the 200 foot drop into water at the

continued on p. 4

think short

monitored activities of underground military newspapers in Okinawa, Iwakuni, and Yokosuka. The Navy used a network of informants to get subscription lists and financial records of these papers.[113]

Despite harassment, several papers grew fairly large. Larger circulation invited even tighter surveillance by military authorities. *Gigline*, published in El Paso, Texas, by GIs for Peace, was another victim of military disruption. The paper's cartoonist was transferred, without advance notice, from the United States to an infantry unit in West Germany. The editor was ordered to Vietnam on short notice. Court-martial papers were drawn against a soldier who distributed *Gigline* on a post.[114]

The Ally, published in Berkeley, California, boasted a circulation of 50,000 among GIs stationed on the West Coast and in the Pacific. Distribution was continually under seige. When a soldier in Vietnam asked permission to distribute *The Ally*, he was transferred to a remote post. At this new post he asked again for permission to distribute the paper and received no answer. Three hundred copies of one issue sent to the soldier were opened in transit. When they did arrive, the soldier's platoon sergeant confiscated them. The GI finally distributed these copies but never received any of the subsequent issues mailed to him. A private at Fort Hood who distributed *The Ally* was court-martialed and sentenced to six months hard labor for distributing unauthorized publications. His sentence was then suspended, and he was discharged from the army as unsuitable for service. Another private arrested for distributing *The Ally* was court-martialed, fined, and shipped to Vietnam. Marine distributors of the paper at Iwakuni, Japan, were interrogated by the Criminal Investigation Division (CID) of military intelligence after receiving large shipments of *The Ally*. The marines, in turn, complained that their mail had been illegally opened. Their commanding officer held that the papers had been damaged in transit, and it was his duty to inspect any such damage. In Korea, the CID instructed mail clerks to impound shipments of *The Ally*. Many subscribers in Korea never received copies of the paper at all or received copies that had been opened and resealed.[115]

Unless an underground military newspaper had wide distribution, such as the one enjoyed by *The Ally*, control over the paper was usually in the hands of the local commanding officer. Occasionally, however, a campaign against a small paper betrayed evidence of collusion among military and outside government agencies. On July 1, 1970, military agents of the Office of Security and Investigations (OSI) used a warrant to search for marijuana in order to ransack the office of *Broken Arrow*. This was the newspaper of the American Servicemen's Union at Selfridge Air Force Base in Michigan. No marijuana was found, but the newspaper's files and the original copy for one issue were confiscated, along with a collection of civilian alternative newspapers, including *The Guardian, Fifth Estate*, and *Seed*. The newspapers were declared contraband, in violation of an Air Force regulation controlling handbills, posters, and similar written material. Two servicemen mentioned in the seized *Broken Arrow* were subsequently searched. Three months later, five civilian women were arrested for distributing issues of the newspaper on the base. The military police took them to the OSI, which delivered them to the local FBI. They were charged with trespassing on federal property.[116]

In most cases, punishment of military personnel was intended to intimidate other writers and publishers. Sentences were often suspended or replaced with transfers. The suspended sentence warned that disciplinary action was always possible for dissidents. Sometimes sentences were carried out, however, as in the case of SP 4 Harold Muskat of Fort Dix, N.J. On May 1, 1969, he was arrested for distributing *The Bond*, then sentenced to six months at hard labor, reduced in rank, and fined.[117]

CONGRESSIONAL DISSIDENTS BANNED

In 1970, the Secretary of the Army affirmed that military personnel had the right of access to unauthorized media, even if the distributor was a civilian. This followed a decision involving twelve civilians arrested for distributing *The Bond*

LINK

THE SERVICEMAN'S LINK TO PEACE
1029 Vermont Avenue NW, Room 200
Washington D C 20005 (202) 638-4126

☮M

THE BEST & THE WORST

25¢ Donation	July 1969	Washington, D. C.	Free to Servicemen

A CALL TO RESIST ILLEGITIMATE AUTHORITY
AN INDICTMENT AGAINST THE U.S. GOVERNMENT, THE ARMED SERVICES AND ITS INDUSTRIAL ALLIES

By Roger Priest, U.S. Navy

WASHINGTON, D.C. -- As a U.S. citizen and as a human being I wish to expose the illegality and immorality of the unnecessary war in Vietnam. I specifically charge the U. S. government, the Armed Services and its industrial allies collectively and individually with the crime of waging aggressive war crimes against humanity, and with specific violations of the laws of war.

Article VI of the Constitution states that the Constitution and treaties made under the Authority of the United States shall be the Supreme law of the land. Therefore if members of the U.S. government, the Armed Services and its industrial allies have broken any international law, then they are liable to prosecution by U.S. courts under Article VI of the Constitution. I charge that the U.S. government, the Armed Services and its industrial allies have broken international laws and established personal responsibility for these criminal actions.

The Nuremberg Principles define a "crime against peace" as the "planning, preparation, initiation or waging of a war of aggression or a war in violation of international treaties, agreements or assurances." A state of war exists in Vietnam where Vietnamese and Americans are killed almost everyday in armed conflict. The war in Vietnam is a war of aggression on the part of the U.S. government, the Armed Services and its industrial allies. Article 51 of the United Nations Charter states that members of the United Nations have the right of individual or collective self-defense if an armed attack occurs against a member of the United Nations. All other acts of war are acts of aggression. This means that the United States would have the legal right to intervene in Vietnam if there was an armed attack upon Vietnam by military forces that crossed an international boundary. This is the only justification for armed intervention.

The United States government has accused the government of Ho Chi Minh of aggression against the government of South Vietnam. For these actions if they did exist, to be defined as aggressive actions, North and South Vietnam must exist as separate countries. North and South Vietnam have never existed as separate countries. The current separation is the result of temporary zoning of the two belligerents of France and the Vietminh after the French-Indochinese War as of 1954. The zoning was only to be temporary. The two zones were to be reunited in 1956 pending elections. Elections the U.S. government never allowed, because Ho Chi Minh had become so popular a national hero that he would win free elections by a big margin (80 per cent, President Eisenhower estimated in his memoirs). The war in Vietnam, then is a civil war, a war between two belligerents indigenous to the same country. Therefore North Vietnam cannot be guilty of acts of aggression against South Vietnam as defined by the United Nations Charter because "armed attack" has never been carried across international boundaries.

There is no way to peace. Peace is the way.

OM, July, 1969.

and *SPD News* at Fort Dix. The court ruled that the civilians were on property open to civilians, and, therefore, they were not violating regulations.[118] Around the same time, Joel Polin, an anti-war activist, had petitioned Fort Bragg,N.C., authorities for permission to distribute a reprint of the *Congressional Record* quoting Senators Eugene McCarthy, George McGovern, and Vance Hartke on the Vietnam war. When Fort Bragg authorities refused, Polin petitioned the Secretary of the Army, citing Army regulations: "A commander may not prevent distribution of a publication simply because he does not like its contents." After a year's delay, the Secretary of the Army agreed to permit Polin to distribute the leaflets, although he was allowed to do so for only one hour.[119]

THE CASE OF ROGER PRIEST

During the spring of 1969, the Navy took action against Journalist Seaman Apprentice Roger Priest. This action was significant because it indicated the military's willingness to openly restrict press freedoms when no other disciplinary avenues were available. Priest, assigned to the Office of Navy Information at the Pentagon, published the first issue of *OM, The Servicemen's Newsletter* on April 1, 1969. Within two hours of its appearance, Priest was reassigned to the Washington Navy Yard.[120] One month later, after the second issue came out, Priest found himself under surveillance. The Navy assigned twenty-five intelligence officers to follow him and arranged with the Washington, D.C., sanitation department to have his garbage inspected.[121] Priest made sure never to waver from the strictest interpretation of military regulations when performing his military duties. He was well aware of how minor infractions were used to silence dissent.

On June 1, the third issue of *OM* appeared. It contained a parable about a hog dirtying a stream and ended with the line: "L. Mendel Rivers, get your ass out of that stream." Five days later, Rivers, then chairman of the House Armed Services Committee, wrote Rear Admiral Means Johnston of the Navy Department that *OM* "reflects a gross abuse of the constitutional right of free speech."[122] Rivers asked what actions would be taken against Priest. On June 20, Johnston replied that the Judge Advocate General had ruled that in all probability "offenses have been committed by Seaman Priest arising out of his publication and dissemination of a publication primarily for the consumpton of military personnel."[123] Fourteen charges were filed against Priest, including disclosure and publication of privileged information, solicitation of desertion, sedition, disloyalty, and wrongful use of "contemptuous words against L. Mendel Rivers."[124] The last charge was later dropped. Priest was eventually convicted of promoting disloyalty and disobedience.

The case of Roger Priest was significant because the Armed Forces could not prosecute him on other than First Amendment grounds. Priest wrote, published, and distributed *OM* entirely on his own time, using privately owned facilities. Several times the Navy attempted to entrap Priest by having seamen ask him for copies of the paper while he was on duty, forcing him to violate base regulations.[125] Priest always refused. Because Priest's publishing activities were not related to his military duty, his lawyers argued that charges be dismissed, citing a Supreme Court ruling prohibiting courts-martial for activities that were not service-connected.

At the original hearing, the trial judges dismissed the charges of soliciting sedition and desertion. These charges were reinstated, however, on the order of higher Navy authorities. Apparently, because of Mendel Rivers, the military was willing to defy Defense Department directives and the Constitution in open denial of press freedoms to military personnel.[126] The Roger Priest case is evidence that the freedom guaranteed to military personnel by the Constitution and supported by Defense Department directives is often arbitrarily violated by military authorities.

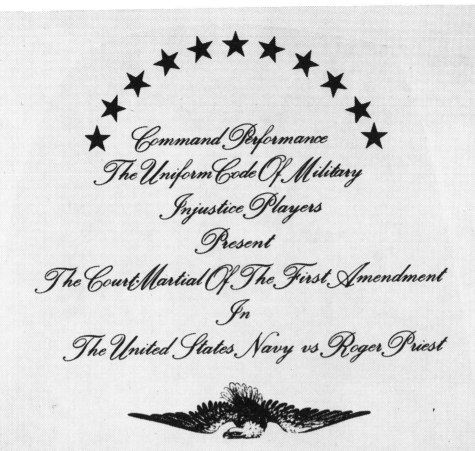

Command Performance

The Uniform Code Of Military

Injustice Players

Present

The Court-Martial Of The First Amendment

In

The United States Navy vs Roger Priest

with:

Roger Priest ✦✦✦✦✦✦✦✦ as the Defendent

David Rein, Lt. Gary Brown

and Lt. James Bailey ✦✦✦✦ as the Defense Attorneys

Captain B. Raymond Perkins ✦✦✦✦ as the Judge

Commander Thomas Jefferson Jimmerson

and Lt. Chesney Floyd ✦✦✦ as the Prosecution Attorneys

Rear Admiral George P. Koch ✦✦✦ as the Commandant
Washington Naval District

✦ and introducing **Allen Ginsberg** leading the **OM** chant

Tickets can be purchased from the Roger Priest Defense Committee rm. 200
1029 Vermont Ave. N.W. Washington DC 20005 or call (202) 683-4126
★★★★★★★★★★★★★★★

Rehearse for the Apocalypse

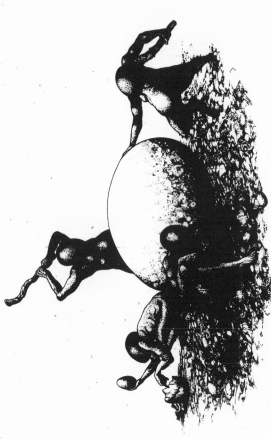

YES FOLKS! NOW YOU CAN BE THE FIRST ON YOUR BLOCK TO EXPERIENCE THE ECOLOGICAL DISASTER. WHY WAIT TILL 1980? DON'T LET THE FUTURE TAKE YOU BY SURPRISE. PREPARE NOW FOR THE END OF CIVILIZATION. REHEARSE FOR THE APOCALYPSE. HERE ARE A FEW SUGGESTIONS:

Better start preparing your pallette and stomach for the fare of the 80's.

* Mix detergent with everything you eat and drink. There's already quite a bit but there will be a lot more in the future.

* Learn how to digest grass and other common plants.

* Start fattening your dog, cat, parakeet and guppies for the main course of the future.

* Develop a taste for grubs and insects - your ancestors weren't too proud to lift a rock for their dinner.

* Practice starving.

* Every night before bedtime drink a glass of industrial and organic waste on the rocks (with mixer if you prefer).

Appreciating that most services and products will disappear over the next ten to twenty years, we suggest this little dry run:

* Turn off your gas
* Turn off your water
* Turn off your telephone
* Turn off your heat
* Turn off your electricity

Sit naked on the floor and repeat this chant: PROGRESS IS OUR MOST IMPORTANT PRODUCT, PROGRESS IS OUR...

And as the final crisis approaches there's no better

time to start hoarding. Start buying things you'll need after the Fall on credit - after the collapse no one will bother with collecting debts.

* While on the subject: start thinking about creative new uses for money since its present function will soon end. Remember, paper - particularly tissue - will be in short supply.

* Think about creative new uses for other potentially obsolete things like electric can openers, televisions, brassieres, toilets, alarm clocks, automobiles, etc.

* Accustom yourself to human body odor.

* Now is the time to learn a trade for the future - practice making arrowheads and other implements out of stone. Advanced students should start experimenting with bronze.

* For those of you who are investment minded, buy land, but you'd better leave enough bread to also buy a small arsenal to defend your property with. Remember Victory Gardens? Plant your Survival Garden now!

* Better quit smoking - or rip off a tobacco warehouse.

* Stockpile useful items like matches, safety pins, thread and needles, condoms, etc.

* Learn how to shoot a bow and arrow.

* Start preparing for the fashions of the future. You girls might take a hint from the heroines of monster films and start tearing your clothing in tasteful but strategically located tatters in order to create the Fay Wray look of tomorrow. Those less frivolous minded among you should start cultivating your body hair. (Remember a naked ape is a cold ape)

* You housewives had better learn how to maim and kill with a vegematic.

* Finally everyone should buy a boy scout manual - or in lieu of that, buy a boy scout.

SO IN FACING THE WORLD OF TOMORROW REMEMBER: BUILD FOR THE FUTURE AND CONTEMPLATE SUICIDE.

INTO THE EIGHTIES

In 1969, Tom Forcade of the Underground Press Syndicate predicted that soon there would be "a daily underground paper in every city and a weekly in every town."[127] Although that optimism proved unfounded, a few underground newspapers are still going strong. The Underground Press Syndicate is now the Alternative Press Syndicate, a clearinghouse and advocate for many remaining papers and publisher of *Alternative Media* magazine. Most surviving publications are aligned with particular liberation movements and are still under siege. Shipments of *Akwesasne Notes*, for example, a paper of the Iroquois Nation in upstate New York, were temporarily blocked by state and federal agents. Full-scale harassment of the Socialist Workers Party, the American Indian movement, the women's movement, and the anti-nuclear movement indicated that intelligence operations have not been curtailed. Out of the Department of Energy came the Federal Response Plan for Peacetime Nuclear Emergencies, giving the FBI authority over those who might pose a threat to nuclear developments. This has been in effect for several years.[128]

In 1978 the *People's Voice*, a Dallas community paper, began covering an anti-nuclear coalition's efforts to stop nuclear power implementation in Texas. Freedom of Information Act documents reveal that not only the Armadillo Coalition but the *People's Voice* and its publisher (the community organization Bois D'Arc Patriots) were under surveillance by the Dallas FBI office and the Bureau of Alcohol, Tobacco and Firearms (BATF). A BATF memo dated November 27, 1978, reports that a *People's Voice* editor and reporter met with the Dallas BATF group supervisor in response to rumors that they were under investigation. The editor disclaimed any connection with an "anti-nuclear power" activist she knew was under investigation and with other activities under the bureau's jurisdiction. The memo—one of a series documenting investigation of the Bois D'Arc Patriots—goes on to report that the the reporter was told "that BATF is not performing such investigations and does not investigate groups or persons

154

because of group membership. [Reporter's name blacked out] said that he assumed that BATF was conducting a tax investigation. He was told that BATF investigates violations of the gun control act, explosives laws and illegal liquor. He appeared not to believe. In summary, neither newsman (sic) was told the substance of our investigation and all questions were answered in general terms."[129]

On June 8, 1979, a memorandum from the FBI Director lists jurisdictional reasons the Dallas FBI office should join the BATF investigation, citing sections of the Atomic Energy Act. It also indicates that the Deputy Attorney General for Emergency Programs, the Secret Service, the Department of Energy and the Nuclear Regulatory Commission should receive data gathered in the investigation.[130]

In addition, the FBI and BATF are working with private energy corporations to stifle anti-nuclear dissent. A May 21, 1979, BATF memorandum on the investigation of the Armadillo Coalition reports: "On May 21, 1979, a meeting was held at the offices of Texas Utilities Generating Company, 2001 Bryan Tower, Dallas, Texas. The following officers of that organization attended the meeting, along with Special Agents [*blacked out*] These officers were advised of the status of this investigation and told what our needs would be as far as protection of the Comanche Peak Steam Electric Station on June 10th was concerned. They again said that the entire resources of their company would be at ATF's disposal . . ."[131] Following the 1980 elections, the government appears to be moving to legitimize and expand the old powers of the intelligence agencies. On April 15, 1981, President Reagan pardoned former FBI officials W. Mark Felt and Edward S. Miller after their conviction for authorizing illegal break-ins in 1972 and 1973. Reagan commended their work against dissident groups, saying they helped "bring an end to the terrorism that was threatening our nation."[132] Because each Presidential administration rewrites history to accommodate its immediate interests, the characterization of dissent of the early 1970s as terrorist signals that dissidents will face serious harassment again.

On March 9, 1981, the ghost of COINTELPRO appeared in reports of proposed revisions in Executive Order 12036, concerning intelligence. Among these revisions are those that return to the FBI almost all the powers it used to disrupt underground newspapers. Citizen recourse and Congressional oversight are all but eliminated, and the protection of civil liberties, mandated by the original Carter Executive Order and Congressional action, are compromised in the interest of the "acquisition of essential information," (Section 2-102). Section 2-201 gives the Attorney General the power to approve by category—rather than by individual case—a wide range of covert intelligence activity without the necessity of obtaining a warrant. This includes wire-tapping, physical searches, mail surveillance, physical surveillance, break-ins, covert participation in organizations, and the collection, storage and dissemination of information on individuals and organizations. A restriction on indirect participation in prohibited or illegal activities is eliminated.[133]

Action by the Reagan administration is being paralleled in both houses of Congress, where legislation and subcommittee hearings aim to remove restraints on intelligence agencies by restricting access to information about them. The Intelligence Identities Protection Act, killed in committee in 1980, was reintroduced in 1981. It calls for prosecuting of unclassified information about intelligence agencies if that information reveals the workings of an agency. The bill's specific target is the *Covert Action Information Bulletin*, which exercises its Constitutional right in disseminating unclassified information. While the bill sweeps wide in an effort to encompass all publication about intelligence activity, its proponents claim that it is intended to protect "mainstream" journalists while permitting the prosecution of dissident journals opposed to intelligence activities.[134] Representative Henry Hyde expressed the view that such journals should not be "permitted to hide" behind the First Amendment.[135]

Representatives in both houses have also announced their intention to propose new charters for the FBI and CIA that would expand their powers. Advocates say a major component of any new charter must exempt intelligence agencies from the provisions of the Freedom of Information Act. On May 4, 1981, Attorney General William French Smith rescinded a requirement that agencies must show that disclosure of information under the Act would be "demonstrably harmful" in order to withhold it.[136] Under the new policy, the Justice Department will defend all agency decisions to withhold information, thereby subverting the intent of the Act and encouraging noncompliance.

Congress is also setting up investigative subcommittees to search out possible links between domestic dissident activity and international terrorist organizations. While FBI Director William Webster was stating that there "was no real evidence" "of direct, deliberate Soviet domination or control or instigation of terrorist activity,"[137] friendly witness Arnaud de Borchgrave testified in the first day of hearings by the Senate Subcommittee on Security and Terrorism that the Soviet Union was involved in "the manipulation of the Western media" and had a "covert role in promoting the anti-nuclear lobby."[138] In seconding this testimony, subcommittee chairman Sen. Jeremiah Denton sent a message that any dissident writing or activity could be interpreted as linked to the Soviet Union or to foreign terrorists, thereby justifying intelligence action. Private advisory groups with links to the Reagan administration have joined this latest round of naming names. An organization called Accuracy in Media, whose newsletter is edited by Reagan supporter Reed Irvine, has recommended an investigation of the Pacifica radio network and a cut-off of federal funding because it "provides a platform for communists."[139] A report by the conservative Heritage Foundation, authored by Security and Terrorism Subcommittee aide Samuel T. Francis, suggests that *Mother Jones*, a survivor of the underground newspaper movement of the 1960s, be targeted for investigation.[140]

On May 3, 1981, over 50,000 people marched on the Pentagon to protest U.S. military aid to El Salvador. It was the largest demonstration of its kind since the Vietnam War. On May 4, Attorney General Smith announced his directive supporting the withholding of information requested under the Freedom of Information Act. Once again widespread popular dissent is being heard in the land. And the mechanisms to suppress that dissent are once again in place.

Published by the RED MOUNTAIN TRIBE Volume 2 Number 14 Issue 40 April 10-17, 1970 THE BAY AREA (its standard)

If it takes a BLOOD BATH let's get it over with. No more appeasement.

Ronald Reagan

Governor State of California

SABOTAGING
THE DISSIDENT PRESS
by Angus Mackenzie

The American public has learned in the last few years a great deal about the government's surveillance of the left during the Vietnam War era. The report of the Senate Select Committee on Intelligence (the Church committee) first suggested how widely the government had been involved in planting informants inside New Left groups, propagating false information about these groups, and using a variety of tactics to disrupt their activities. That such tactics were also used on a vast scale against dissenting magazines and the underground press, however, has not been reported in a comprehensive way. The story has lain scattered in a hundred places. Now, documents obtained by editors and writers under the Freedom of Information Act, and interviews with former intelligence agents, make it possible, for the first time, to put together a coherent—though not necessarily complete—account of the federal government's systematic and sustained violation of the First Amendment during the late 1960s and early 1970s.

The government's offensive against the underground press primarily involved three agencies—the CIA, the FBI, and the Army. In many cases, their activities stemmed from what they could claim were legitimate concerns. The CIA's Operation CHAOS, for example, was set up to look into the foreign connections of domestic dissidents; however, it soon exceeded its mandate and became part of the broad attack on the left and on publications that were regarded as creating a climate disruptive of the war effort. At its height, the government's offensive may have affected more than 150 of the roughly 500 underground publications that became the nerve centers of the antiwar and countercultural movements.

A telling example of this offensive was the harassment of Liberation News Service, which, when opposition to the Vietnam War was building, played a key role in keeping the disparate parts of the antiwar movement informed. By 1968, the FBI had assigned three informants to penetrate the news service, while nine other informants regularly reported on it from the outside. Their reports were forwarded to the U.S. Army's Counterintelligence Branch, where an analyst kept tabs on LNS founders Ray Mungo and Marshall Bloom, and to the Secret Service, the Internal Revenue Service, the Navy, the Air Force, and the CIA. The FBI also attempted to discredit and break up the news service through various counterintelligence activities, such as trying to make LNS appear to be an FBI front, to create friction among staff members, and to burn down the LNS office in Washington while the staff slept upstairs. Before long, the CIA, too, joined the offensive; one of its recruits began filing reports on the movements of LNS staff members while reporting for the underground press to establish his cover as an underground journalist.

The CIA was apparently the first federal agency to plan actions against domestic publications. Its Operation CHAOS grew out of an investigation of *Ramparts* magazine, which during the late 1960s was perhaps the leading national publication of the left. In early 1967, *Ramparts* was preparing to publish an exposé on the CIA's funding of the U.S. National Student Association and on various foundations the agency used as conduits for that funding. The CIA got wind of the article in January 1967, two months before the planned March publication date. Viewing the article as "an attack on CIA in particular and the administration in general," the agency started to monitor the activities of *Ramparts* editors, ostensibly to ascertain whether they had contacts with hostile intelligence services. The CIA's Directorate of Plans (its "dirty tricks" department) assigned to counterintelligence agent Richard Ober the task of "pulling together information on *Ramparts*, including any evidence of subversion [and] devising proposals for counteraction." While those proposals remain secret, several details relating to the *Ramparts* operation have become known.

On February 1, an associate of Ober's met with Thomas Terry, assistant to the commissioner of the Internal Revenue Service, to request that the IRS review *Ramparts'* corporate tax returns to determine who the magazine's backers were. Terry agreed to do so. Subsequently, Ober's office provided the IRS with "detailed informant information" about *Ramparts* backers, whom the IRS was requested to investigate for possible tax violations. Ober's investigation of the magazine uncovered no "evidence of subversion" or ties to foreign intelligence agencies. By August, however, it had produced a computerized listing of several hundred Americans, about fifty of whom were the subject of detailed files.

In August, too, Ober's mandate was expanded as the CIA, responding to pressure from President Johnson, initiated a massive and largely still-secret program of spying on and analyzing political protest—that is, Operation CHAOS. The underground press was one of its targets, the others being antiwar groups, radical youth organizations, black militants, and deserters and draft resisters. CHAOS, of course, raised special problems because it violated a clause in the agency's charter prohibiting the CIA from performing any "internal security function." To give a semblance of legality to the operation, the same justification was used as in the *Ramparts* investigation—namely, that the motive was to search out possible foreign funding or control.

In tracking the press, the CIA was able to count on help from the Army, with which, CHAOS files state, "Direct operational discussions on joint agent operations have been held." Ralph Stein directed the "New Left" desk for the Army's Counterintelligence Analysis Branch in Arlington, Virginia. The branch kept track of underground periodicals and maintained a microfilm crossfile on writers and editors affiliated with them. Stein got most of his information from public sources, but some of it came from classified intelligence reports which, he says, were provided by FBI and Army infiltrators. "Their information was too good, too inside," to have come from public source material, Stein recalled in a recent interview.

In late 1967, Stein was dispatched to CIA headquarters to brief liaison officer Jim Ludlum and others (presumably from Ober's office) on underground and student publications. He found, however, that the CIA men already knew a great deal about the subject. Two questions were foremost in their minds. They wanted to know all about "the ideas and beliefs of the individuals who produced these publications," Stein recalled, and about foreign financing of such prominent publications as *Ramparts* and a host of small underground papers. Stein's response to the latter question was, presumably, unsatisfactory. "Far from being financed by any hostile power abroad," he commented recently, "the people who were putting out these papers were actually using their lunch money, and we were able to prove this." After his briefing session at the CIA, Stein returned to his Arlington office, where he remarked that he thought the CIA was not supposed to engage in domestic surveillance. Shortly thereafter, he was relieved of his liaison duties with the agency, which were taken over by a superior.

Like Stein, Ober found no evidence to support the suspicion that domestic dissidents were being financed or controlled by foreign powers. And, to Ober's credit, his office consistently reported that the antiwar and black nationalist movements were, in fact, responses to domestic political and economic frustrations. But the White House could not abandon what had by now become an *idée fixe* and—particularly after Richard Nixon's election in 1968—it pushed the CIA to probe further into domestic politics. The collection of names continued apace. (By 1973, when CHAOS was converted into the CIA's International Terrorism Group, the computerized list of Americans that Ober had begun to compile in 1967 had grown to include 300,000 names.)

In May 1969, as surveillance activities increased, then-CIA director Richard Helms stated in a memo to field offices that "Operational priority of CHAOS activities in the field is in the highest category, ranking with Soviet and Chicom [Chinese Communist]." While the agency had formerly relied on FBI personnel, it now began recruiting outsiders for CHAOS undercover work. One such recruit was Sal Ferrera, mentioned in a December 27, 1977, *New York Times* article as having worked as a CIA operative in Washington, D.C., and Paris. The details of Ferrara's association with Operation CHAOS are reported here for the first time. They provide a glimpse into just how the CIA spied on the American press.

Ferrera grew up in Chicago, studied revolutionary theory at Loyola University, and in 1969 moved to Washington, D.C., where he made contact with local journalists writing for underground publications. He attended early meetings of the newly founded *Quicksilver Times*, which quickly became the city's leading crusader against the Vietnam War. When the first issue came out on June 16, 1969, Ferrera's name was on the masthead. He participated in editorial decisions and represented the paper at various functions, and he continued to work in the underground press at home and abroad until 1974.

At some point not yet known he also went to work for CHAOS, his underground press connections providing him with impeccable "radical credentials." Wherever there was radical activity, Ferrera seemed to be there. Between January and April 1970, he interviewed Abbie Hoffman, Jerry Rubin, and other members of the Chicago Seven, as well as their lawyer, William Kunstler. In Washington, he became acquainted with Karl Hess, who worked for *The Libertarian* magazine, and soon took to dropping in to visit Hess's office in the basement of the Institute for Policy Studies, a center for antiwar activities.

During the 1971 May Day antiwar demonstration in Washington, Ferrera took photographs and reported on the event for College Press Service, an antiwar syndication service; he may well have been the agent mentioned in the Rockefeller Commission's hearings on the CIA as having covered the demonstration for the agency. He also appears to have been the source of two reports to the CIA regarding staff members of Liberation News Service. In late April, when Ferrera was still working in the *Quicksilver* office, an LNS editor stopped in to ask if LNS staff members who planned to come down from New York for May Day could lodge there. A CHAOS informant's report, dated April 25 and released to LNS editor

Andrew Marx under the FOIA, refers to this visit. A second report lists all LNS staff members who attended the May Day demonstration.

Ferrera subsequently went to live in Paris, where he wrote articles on radical student politics for LNS and College Press Service. In 1972, the CIA assigned Ferrera and another agent to monitor the activities of Philip Agee, who was then living in Paris and writing *Inside the Company*, his exposé of CIA operations in Latin America. Ferrera returned to the U.S. (and legally changed his name) in 1975, the year Agee's book appeared. When interviewed for this article, he denied his relationship with the CIA.

Ferrera's activities were not unique, as documents obtained by the Center for National Security Studies, a public-interest group based in Washington, D.C., make clear. In one memorandum a former CIA case officer for domestic CHAOS agents is quoted as saying that several such agents were active in this county "anywhere from months to years." Their activities belie the contention of the Church committee report, based on the claims of the CIA itself, that CHAOS agents operated in the U.S. primarily for training and cover purposes.

Four months after CHAOS was set up, the CIA initiated another domestic spying program. Run by the agency's Office of Security, it was dubbed Project Resistance—and it soon came up with a novel and quite effective means of shutting down dissident publications. Created in the wake of a program begun in February 1967 and designed narrowly to protect CIA recruiters on college campuses, Resistance soon became a nationwide probe of campus and non-campus dissident groups, paying special attention to the underground press. The Church committee report stated that Project Resistance was "a broad effort to obtain general background for predicting violence, which might have created threats to CIA installations, recruiters or contractors. . . ." Files obtained by the Center for National Security Studies, however, make it clear that Project Resistance's main purpose was to infiltrate the underground press, and that it did so routinely, sometimes through local police informers.

In late 1968, a Resistance analyst filed the following

memo:

> A modern phenomenon which has evolved in the last
> three or four years is the vast growth of the Under
> ground Press. Underground means of mass communica-
> tion utilized to avoid suppression by legal authority
> and/or attribution is not new to this age, but its volume
> is and the apparent freedom and ease in which filth,
> slanderous and libelous statements, and what appear to
> be almost treasonous anti-establishment propaganda is
> allowed to circulate is difficult to rationalize.

Then he suggested a novel strategy for silencing such "anti-establishment propaganda." The underground papers, he wrote, "are not a quality press. Eight out of 10 would fail if a few phonograph record companies stopped advertising in them." Since Resistance, like CHAOS, was nominally a spy operation, and since, again nominally, the CIA was prohibited from performing any "internal security function," the CIA did not itself feel comfortable carrying out such a program. The FBI, however, felt no such inhibitions.

In January 1969, four months after the Resistance agent had filed his memo on the underground press, the FBI's San Francisco office wrote to headquarters in Washington and to the FBI's New York office, asserting that financial "assistance" from Columbia Records—i.e., advertisements in the *Berkeley Barb* and other underground papers—"appears to be giving active aid and comfort to enemies of the United States." The San Francisco office suggested that the FBI should use its contacts to persuade Columbia Records to stop advertising in the underground press.

One of the first publications to feel the effect of this strategy was the *Free Press*, an alternative paper in Washington, D.C. Its February 1 issue was the last to carry Columbia record ads, a vital source of revenue. By the end of the year the paper was dead. In Wisconsin, the six-paper Kaleidoscope underground chain, created for the express purpose of obtaining ads from New York record companies, also succumbed. In a recent interview, Marc Knops, the editor of the *Madison Kaleidoscope*, which survived briefly on local ads, said that when the record companies pulled out, "The bottom fell out of the ad market. By autumn 1969 there was no income. *Kaleidoscope* was gone as a functioning chain." (In 1970 the former chain's Milwaukee paper, also surviving on local ads, was the target of another effort by the FBI's local office, which attempted—but failed—to use "public exposure" to gain the dismissal of two professors who frequently contributed to the underground paper. Similar, more successful efforts were directed against professors at the University of South Alabama who had contributed to the radical *Rearguard*.)

Deprived of most of its record ads, the *Berkeley Barb* survived on lewd sex ads. At the *Barb*, as elsewhere, editors and staff had no clear indication of why a major source of revenue had suddenly evaporated. Columbia Records has declined to comment.

Throughout the country, other FBI offices employed similar tactics to silence the dissident press. When headquarters ordered the Detroit office to "neutralize" the *South End* and the *State News*, the student papers at Wayne State and Michigan State universities respectively, the office sent anonymous letters of protest to local businesses that advertised in them. A more limited campaign was waged against *The Tech*, the student paper at Massachusetts Institute of Technology.

Another bureau ploy used against college papers consisted of anonymously mailing their most controversial articles to funding sources and other influential persons, including state legislators, college trustees, and "friendly news media." "Items submitted should be extremely radical on their face, use profanity or be repulsive in nature," J. Edgar Hoover stated in a directive to fourteen field offices in May 1968.

The FBI also enlisted the assistance of local banks. In Cincinnati, the branch office obtained transaction records for two underground papers, the *Independent Eye* and the *Queen City Express*, helping it to identify advertisers and contributors. "As information is gathered," a memo dated July 8, 1970 stated, "it is believed there will be opportunities to suggest counterintelligence action against individuals and groups who are giving financial support to these publications."

Showing initiative, in 1970 the El Paso office proposed a "possible counterintelligent [sic] action" designed to silence the editor of the underground *The Sea Turtle and the Shark;* the idea was to publicize his alleged past criminal activities and "dependence upon various welfare programs." Eventually the editor was arrested for selling an "obscene newspaper" to a minor after the FBI had supplied information to local authorities.

In addition to these comparatively restrained strategies, the FBI also instigated violent acts. In San Diego, for instance, the paramilitary Secret Army Organization, led by FBI informant Howard Godfrey, assaulted the offices and staff of the *Street Journal* on December 25, 1969. By January of 1971, the commune that published the *Journal* had broken up. FBI documents released under the FOIA show for the first time that the Secret Army Organization's operations extended as far east as Wisconsin, where the organization threatened to kidnap Mike Fellner, editor of the radical Madison paper *Takeover.*

In some cities, when direct attacks proved unsuccessful, the government set up its own phony news service which, so long as it was unexposed, provided a means of penetrating the left; once exposed, it cast suspicion on legitimate underground reporters and helped to create a feeling of paranoia. The Army started *Midwest News* in Chicago, according to former intelligence officer Ralph Stein; in San Francisco, the FBI set up Pacific International News Service. The head of the FBI's San Francisco office at the time, Charles Bates—he is now a reporter for KGO-TV in San Francisco—said recently that he did not specifically recall Pacific International, but added that front operations of that kind "would have been fine if it weren't put down in writing." A spokesman for the San Francisco field office refused to confirm or deny the bureau's use of the news service. Meanwhile, on the East Coast, the FBI operated New York Press Service under the direction of Louis Salzberg. NYPS offered its services to left-wing publications at attractive rates, soliciting business with a letter that read, in part: "The next time your organization schedules a demonstration, march, picket or office party, let us know in advance. We'll cover it like a blanket and deliver a cost-free sample of our work to your office." NYPS's cover was blown when Salzberg surfaced as a government witness in the Chicago Seven trial, during which it was disclosed that he had been an FBI informant.

The New York field office shrewdly turned this setback into a means of casting suspicion on Liberation News Service. The office prepared an anonymous letter, copies of which were sent to newspapers and antiwar groups, accusing LNS of being an FBI front. "Lns [sic] is in an ideal position to infiltrate the movement at every level," the letter stated. "It has carefully concealed its books from all but a select few. Former employees have openly questioned its sources of operating funds. I shall write to you further on Lns for I (and several others) are taking steps to expose this fraud for what it really is—a government financed front."

Such, then, were the techniques used by the U.S. government to stifle freedom of expression in the late 1960s and early 1970s. These and other violations of American civil liberties, as publicized in the Church committee report, together with the public revulsion that attended its publication, resulting in restrictions on domestic surveillance by the CIA and FBI. Now the removal of those safeguards seems a distinct possibility, at least to judge by the recent report on intelligence issued by the Heritage Foundation and embraced by the Reagan transition team. That report claims that "The threat to the internal security of the Republic is greater today than at any time since World War II" and recommends resurrecting the standing internal security committees in Congress and, once again, permitting the FBI and CIA to spy on dissidents, including journalists.

If Reagan officials do go ahead and propose such measures, they will undoubtedly argue that guarantees can be established to prevent surveillance from getting out of hand. But if the experience of the Johnson and Nixon years is any guide, even programs which begin quite modestly can expand far beyond their original mandate.

FIEFDOMS OF INFORMATION

In my two-year-long effort to obtain federal agency files on underground publications, I learned almost as much about how the Freedom of Information Act works—or doesn't work—as I did about the means by which the government sought to suppress dissent in the 1960s and 1970s. I found, above all, that while some agencies were quite cooperative, the CIA and FBI proved adept at keeping their information to themselves.

In requesting FBI counterintelligence files and the entire "New Left Publications" file under the FOIA, I was able to supply the bureau with seventy-eight file numbers relating to forty-seven periodicals (obtained from heavily censored files previously released to editors of publications that no longer exist). Since the most difficult element in any request is identifying documents specifically enough so that the agency can locate them, this should have facilitated a quick response. Instead, the FBI demanded an advance deposit of $1,100 for more than 1,100 hours of search time. My appeal of that payment is still pending.

In the case of the CIA, I was able to supply the agency with four file numbers. After twenty-six days a letter came stating that I would have to agree to unspecified search fees. Nothing then happened until fourteen months later, when a second letter said I would have to deposit $30,000 on a search they estimated would cost a total of $61,501.

The Secret Service, by contrast, waived search-and-copy fees and complied with my request within seventeen days, sending forty censored pages dealing with nineteen newspapers—even though I had been unable to supply any file numbers to the service. Likewise, the Department of Defense attempted to comply with the intent of the act, although, again, I was unable to supply file numbers. Within thirty-two days of my request, the department waived $445.50 in search-and-copy fees. After a search, its Defense Investigative Service determined that it might have records on seventeen of the 500 newspapers on my list.

Supposedly, new teeth were put in the FOIA in 1974. At the time, a House-Senate conference report said that agencies must comply with requests within thirty days, that "fees should not be used for the purpose of discouraging requests," and that withheld files must concern activity within the agency's legal authority. My experience shows that the CIA and the FBI refuse to comply with both the intent and letter of the amended act.

FURTHER READING

Armstrong, David. *A Trumpet to Arms: Alternative Media in America*. Los Angeles: J. B. Tarcher, 1981.

Berlet, Chip. "COINTELPRO," *Alternative Media*. Vol. 10, No. 2, Fall 1978.

Berman, Jerry J., Robert L. Borosage, Morton H. Halperin, and Christine Marwick. *The Lawless State: The Crimes of The U.S. Intelligence Agencies*. New York: Penguin Books, 1976.

Burks, John. "The Underground Press," *Rolling Stone*, No. 43, October 4, 1969.

Cowan, Paul, Nick Egleson, and Nat Hentoff, with Barbara Herbert and Robert Wall. *State Secrets: Police Surveillance in America*. New York: Holt, Rinehart and Winston, 1974.

Forcade, Thomas King, "Obscenity, Who Really Cares?", *Countdown*, 1971.

Fruchter, Norman, "Movement Propaganda and the Culture of the Spectacle," *Liberation*, May, 1971.

Gitlin, Todd. *The Whole World is Watching: Mass Media in the Making & Unmaking of the New Left*. Berkeley: University of California Press, 1980.

Marks, John. *The Search for the Manchurian Candidate*. New York: New York Times Book Co., 1979.

Morgan, Richard E. *Domestic Intelligence; Monitoring Dissent in America*. Austin: University of Texas Press, 1980.

O'Toole, George. "America's Secret Police Network," *Penthouse*, December, 1976.

FOOTNOTES

[1] John Burks, "The Underground Press," *Rolling Stone*, No. 43, Oct. 4, 1969, p. 31.

[2] "Underground Fuck," San Francisco *Express-Times*, Dec. 11, 1968.

[3] "Letter to Our Friends," Philadelphia *Free Press*, Aug. 2, 1970.

[4] Rod Lord, "Letter: Dissent in the Service," *Playboy*, Nov., 1970.

[5] *Final Report of the Select Committee to Study Governmental Operations with Respect to Intelligence Activities*, United States Senate, Supplementary Detailed Staff Reports of Intelligence Activities and Rights of Americans, Book III (Washington, D.C.: U.S. Government Printing Office, 1976), pp. 510-511.

[6] U.S. Senate, Select Committee, *Final Report, Op. Cit.*, p. 734.

[7] *Ibid.*, pp. 923-957.

[8] *Ibid.*, pp. 962-967.

[9] Jerry J. Berman, Robert L. Borosage, Morton H. Halperin, Christine M. Marwick, *The Lawless State* (New York: Penguin Books, 1976), p. 120.

[10] U.S. Senate, Select Committee, *Final Report, Op. Cit.*, pp. 815-817.

[11] *Ibid.*, pp. 818-822.

[12] *Ibid.*, 823-824.

[13] Letter from J. Edgar Hoover to Tolson, DeLoach, Rosen, Bishop, Sullivan, June 20, 1968. Expression Repression File: Freedom of Information Act Document, PEN American Center, pp. 194A-G. (Hereafter cited as FOIA [PEN].)

[14] Berman, et al., *Op. Cit.*, p. 112.

[15] *Ibid.*, pp. 114-120.

[16] *Ibid.*, pp. 119-120.

[17] Memorandum from the Director to SAC, Albany, July 5, 1968, FOIA (PEN), pp. 40-42.

[18] Memorandum from the Director to SAC, Indianapolis, October 4, 1968; and memorandum from SAC, San Antonio, to the Director, January 17, 1969, FOIA (PEN), pp. 132A-C.

[19] Berman, et al., *Op. Cit.*, pp. 140-141.

[20] U.S. Senate, Select Committee, *Final Report, Op. Cit.*, p. 681.

[21] Berman et al., *Op. Cit.*, p. 32.

[22] George O'Toole, "America's Secret Police Network," *Penthouse*, Dec., 1976 (Penthouse Ind. Ltd., New York, 1976).

[23] John Marks, *The Search for the Manchurian Candidate* (New York: New York Times Book Co., 1979) pp. 120-121.

[24] Berman et al., *Op. Cit.*, p. 200.

[25] *Ibid.*, p. 197.

[26] *Ibid.*, p. 200.

[27] *Ibid.*, p. 182.

[28] O'Toole, *Op. Cit.*

[29] *Ibid.*

[30] Thomas King Forcade, "Obscenity, Who Really Cares?," *Countdown*, 1971, p. 160.

[31] "The Members," *Alternative Media*, Vol. 10, No. 2, Fall, 1978, pp. 28-30.

[32] John Burks, "The Underground Press," *Rolling Stone*, No. 43, October 4, 1969, p. 17.

[33] Agis Salpukas, "Underground Papers are Thriving on Campuses and in Cities Across Nation," *New York Times*, April 5, 1970.

[34] Memorandum from SAC, Newark, to the Director, June 3, 1970, FOIA (PEN), p. 65A.

[35] Chip Berlet, "COINTELPRO," *Alternative Media*, Vol. 10, No. 2, Fall, 1978, p. 11.

[36] Thomas King Forcade, "Free Media," (unpublished), 1970.

[37] Berlet, *Op. Cit.*, p. 10.

[38] *Newsletter for Intellectual Freedom*, Vol. XIX, No. 6, Nov., 1970, American Library Association, p. 90.

[39] Agis Salpukas, *Op. Cit.*

[40] Forcade, *Countdown*, p. 163.

[41] Agis Salpukas, *Op. Cit.*

[42] Forcade, *Countdown*, p. 171. (Unless otherwise noted, sources of information on individual publications can be found in the Expression Repression File, PEN American Center, listed under the name of the publication.)

[43] Letter: Reber F. Boult, Jr., ACLU Foundation, Southern Regional Office, Oct. 6, 1970. Expression Repression File: *Great Speckled Bird.*

[44] FBI memoranda to and from SAC, New Orleans, April 16, 1969 through Jan. 21, 1976, FOIA (PEN), pp. 142-189.

[45] *USA vs. Robert Grady Head, Jr., et al.*, Criminal Action No. 32036, Section "C", United States District Court, Eastern District of La., New Orleans Division, Sept. 1, 1970.

[46] Forcade, *Countdown*, p. 166.

[47] Berlet, *Op. Cit.*, p. 12.

[48] "Underground Fuck," *Op. Cit.*

[49] *Ibid.*

[50] Berlet, *Op. Cit.*, p. 12.

[51] SAC, New York, Report: "Underground Press Syndicate," Dec. 10, 1969. FOIA (PEN), pp. 300-307.

[52] Forcade, *Countdown*, pp. 168-169.

[53] Burks, *Op. Cit.*, p. 31.

[54] Berlet, *Op. Cit.*, pp. 11-12.

[55] Memorandum from SAC, Detroit, to the Director, Oct. 13, 1970, FOIA (PEN), pp. 65, 65A, 66.

[56] John Pekkanen. "The Obstinacy of Bill Schanen," *Life*, 1970.

174

[57] U.S. Senate, Select Committee, *Final Report, Op. Cit.*, pp. 30-31.

[58] *Ibid.*

[59] "Underground Fuck," *Op. Cit.*

[60] Forcade, *Countdown*, p. 169.

[61] "Underground Fuck., *Op. Cit.*

[62] Forcade, *Countdown*, p. 168.

[63] Expression Repression File: John Sinclair, (PEN).

[64] "Juche Collective Busted," *Liberated Guardian*, Dec. 14, 1970, pp. 16-18. "Pigs Freak Out," *Juche*, November, 1970, p. 24. " 'Revolutionary' Den Raided," *Record American*, Boston, Nov. 18, 1970, pp. 1, 3, 32.

[65] Expression Repression File B-1: "Repression of the Underground Press" (unpublished).

[66] Doug Baker, Jr., "Why They Got Stoney Burns," *Iconoclast*, Dallas, Nov. 29, Dec. 6, Dec. 13, 1974.

[67] *Ibid.*

[68] FBI memorandum, Dec. 10, 1969, New York, FBI, FOIA (PEN), pp. 300-301.

[69] "Underground Fuck," *Op. Cit.*

[70] "Letter to Our Friends," Philadelphia *Free Press*, August 2, 1970.

[71] Bayard Brunt and Albert V. Gaudiosi, "The New Revolutionaries: Head of Rebel Paper is Central Figure in New Left Here," Philadelphia *Evening Bulletin*, July 28, 1970, pp. A1, B3.

[72] Paul Delaney, "Police Officials Endorse Senate Bills Aimed at Curbing Urban Guerrilla Warfare," *New York Times*, Oct. 7, 1970.

[73] *Hearings Before the Select Committee to Study Governmental Operations with Respect to Intelligence Activities*, U.S. Senate, 94th Congress, First Session, Vol. 6, "Federal Bureau of Investigation," (Washington, D.C.: U.S. Government Printing Office, 1976), Exhibit 69-23, pp. 804-806.

[74] *Resist Newsletter #48*, Dec. 2, 1970, p. 3.

[75] "Repression of the Underground Press," File B-1.

[76] U.S. Senate, Select Committee, *Final Report, Op. Cit.*, p. 824.

[77] *Second City*, Vol. 2, No. 6, 1970.

[78] O'Toole, *Op. Cit.*

[79] U.S. Senate, Select Committee, *Final Report, Op. Cit.*, p. 803.

[80] O'Toole, *Op. Cit.*

[81] CIA memorandum from Howard J. Osborn, Director of Security, to Deputy Director for Support, Feb. 8, 1973, FOIA (PEN), pp. 230-236.

[82] Berlet, *Op. Cit.*, p. 12.

[83] Burks, *Op. Cit.*, p. 30.

[84] "Repression of the Underground Press," File B-1.

[85] *Ibid.*

[86] *Ibid.*

[87] U.S. Senate, Select Committee, *Final Report, Op. Cit.*, p. 30.

[88] "Repression of the Underground Press," File B-1.

[89] *Dallas Morning News*, Oct. 8, 1970.

[90] *New York Times*, March 27, 1971.

[91] Berman et al., *Op. Cit.*, p. 131.

[92] Lew Moores, "FBI Opened Bank Records in Paper Probe," Cincinnati *Post*, March 22, 1979.

[93] FBI memorandum from Washington, D.C., FBI to the Director, March 16, 1970, FOIA (PEN), p. 196F.

[94] FBI memorandum from the Director to Washington, D.C., FBI, March 4, 1970, FOIA (PEN), p. 196B.

[95] FBI memorandum from Washington, D.C., FBI to the Director, July 2, 1973, FOIA (PEN), p. 196H.

[96] Larry Remer, "Targets: *Street Journal* and *Door*," *Alternative Media*, Alternative Press Syndicate.

[97] "Message from the Staff," *San Diego Street Journal*, July 24, 1970.

[98] *Lowell Bergman and Jan Diepersloot and the Peoples' Commune vs. O. J. Roed, et al.*, U.S. District Court, Southern District of California, Case No. 7057 S, Feb. 24, 1970.

[99] "Message from the Staff." *Op. Cit.*

[100] Larry Remer, *Op. Cit.*

[101] *Ibid.*

[102] Memoranda from SAC, San Diego, FOIA (PEN), pp. 190-193.

[103] FBI memorandum from the Director to SAC, Chicago, May 3, 1968, FOIA (PEN), pp. 195A-195E.

[104] Nanzy Beezley, College Press Service, University of Mo. *Maneater*, March 10, 1970.

[105] *The Bond*, Vol. 3, No. 1, New York, Jan. 21, 1969, p. 2.

[106] *Ibid.*, Vol. 3, No. 8, Aug. 25, 1969, p. 3.

[107] *Your Military Left*, Vol. 1, No. 8, San Antonio, Mar. 15, 1970, p. 11.

[108] Stephen G. Gross, "Military News Media Censorship," *Freedom of Information Center Report No. 243* (School of Journalism, University of Missouri at Columbia, June, 1970), p. 5.

[109] *The Repress*, Vol. 1, No. 2, Washington, D.C., Dec. 1969, p. 4.

[110] U.S. Senate, Select Committee, *Final Report, Op. Cit.*, pp. 815-816.

[111] *Ibid.*, pp. 814-816.

[112] *Ibid.*, pp. 816-817.

[113] *Ibid.*, pp. 820-822.

[114] Gross, *Op.Cit.*, p. 6.

[115] Rod Lord, "Letter: Dissent in the Service," *Playboy*, Nov., 1970.

[116] "Air Force Cops Raid Union Paper," *The Bond*, July 22, 1970, p. 5.

176

[117] *The Bond*, May 20, 1970, p. 3.

[118] *Ibid.*, April 22, 1970, p. 3.

[119] "The Army Way," *Playboy*, Feb., 1971.

[120] "Biographical Facts on Roger L. Priest," Priest Defense Committee (unpublished), Expression Repression File A-3.

[121] Philip M. Stern, "Seaman Priest," *The New Republic*, Vol. 162, No. 7, Issue 1877, Feb. 14, 1970.

[122] Letter from L. Mendel Rivers to Rear Admiral Means Johnston, June 6, 1969, Expression Repression File A-3.

[123] Letter from Rear Admiral Means Johnston to L. Mendel Rivers, June 20, 1969, Expression Repression File A-3.

[124] Gross, *Op. Cit.*, p. 7.

[125] Alan Lewis, "First Amendment on Trial," *Argus*, Vol. 5, No. 2, University of Maryland.

[126] Stern, *Op. Cit.*

[127] Burks, *Op. Cit.*, p. 17.

[128] Tim Butz, "Surveillance of the Anti-Nuke Movement," *Public Eye*, Vol. 1, No. 2, April, 1978, pp. 40-43.

[129] BATF memorandum from Dallas groups supervisor to SAC, Dallas BATF district office, November 27, 1978, FOIA (PEN), p. PV-1.

[130] FBI memorandum from the Director to Dallas FBI and San Antonio FBI, June 8, 1979, FOIA (Pen), p. PV-3.

[131] BATF memorandum (No. 3006 0678 2502F) from Dallas groups supervisor to SAC, Dallas BATF district office, May 24, 1979, FOIA (PEN), p. PV-6.

[132] Robert Pear, "President Pardons 2 Ex-FBI Officials in 1970's Break-ins," *The New York Times*, April 16, 1981, p. A-1.

[133] Executive Order 12036, President Jimmy Carter, January 24, 1978; Federal Document 78-2420, filed 1-25-78, published in Federal Register, Vol. 43, No. 18, January 26, 1978. With suggested revisions added by Reagan Administration.

[134] Charles Mohr, "Senate Panel Acts to Narrow Intelligence Identities Bill," *The New York Times*, Sept. 18, 1980, p. A-21.

[135] Charles Mohr, "House Panel Clears Bill to Ban Naming of Covert Agents," *The New York Times*, Sept. 4, 1980.

[136] Philip Taubman, "U.S. Agencies to Get Greater Discretion on Releasing Files," *The New York Times*, May 4, 1981, p. A-1.

[137] Robert Pear, "FBI Director Sees No Evidence Soviet Fosters Terrorism in U.S.," *The New York Times*, April 27, 1981.

[138] Charles Mohr, "Hearing on Terror Opens with Warning on Soviet," *The New York Times*, April 25, 1981, p. A-10.

[139] "Look Who's Tapping the Federal Till," *AIM Report*, Accuracy in Media, Inc., Reed Irvine, ed., Vol. IX, No. 20, October 11, 1980.

[140] George Larner, Jr., "Assault on Terrorism: Internal Security or Witch Hunt?" *The Washington Post*, April 20, 1981, p. A-1.